from **women of faith**

speakers and friends

loved
by God
DEVOTIONAL

52 Encouraging Reminders
that You *are* Seen, Known, *and* Free

TYNDALE
MOMENTUM

An Imprint of
Tyndale House Publishers, Inc.

Visit Women of Faith at www.womenoffaith.com.

Visit Tyndale online at www.tyndale.com.

Visit Tyndale Momentum online at www.tyndalemomentum.com.

TYNDALE, Tyndale Momentum, and the Tyndale Momentum logo are registered trademarks of Tyndale House Publishers, Inc. Tyndale Momentum is an imprint of Tyndale House Publishers, Inc., Carol Stream, Illinois. *Women of Faith* is a registered trademark of Women of Faith LLC.

Designed by Stephen Vosloo

Printed in the United States of America

21	20	19	18	17	16	15
7	6	5	4	3	2	1

Contents

WINTER

You Are Loved by God

Through stories from our own experiences and the pages of Scripture, Women of Faith offers a glimpse into God's delight in women and what he has to say about the places where we feel most vulnerable.

Can anyone see me? Does anyone care? Does what I do matter?

Making your way through the dailiness of life, sometimes it can be hard to tell. God sees. He cares. And it does matter.

You are seen.

If they knew the real me . . .

That little voice inside whispers the fear that keeps you

isolated. But God knows you inside and out. He created you specifically to be *you*.
You are known.

There aren't enough hours in the day.
Jesus offers to carry your schedules and responsibilities and the worries that keep you up at night. He promises restoration, forgiveness, and new life.
You are free.

Every minute of every day, no matter how you feel, the reality is . . .
You are loved.

$\left(\text{SPRING} \right)$

This Is Going to Be Fun!

by Luci Swindoll

Each time he said, "My grace is all you need. My power works best in weakness." So now I am glad to boast about my weaknesses, so that the power of Christ can work through me.

2 CORINTHIANS 12:9

I was driving down a California highway on my way to my job at Mobil Oil when I said, "You know, Lord, I'm not very happy with my life. It's wonderful, but I don't feel like it *matters*. I want to do something significant, but I don't really know what significant means in *my* life. So would you give me something meaningful to do? And when you do, would you say to me (not audibly, of course), 'This is it!' so I don't have to wonder? I would really appreciate that, Lord."

When I arrived at work, I got a call from my brother, Chuck, inviting me to dinner. He said, "The president of a publishing company is going to be there, and I want you to meet him."

So I went. I was talking to this guy about how much I enjoy being single, and he asked me, "Would you write a book about that?"

I heard a voice inside saying, *This is it!* . . . and I thought, *Surely not, Lord. I don't know how to write a book.* The voice said, *Just say yes.* So I did. And the voice said, *Now we're talking. This is going to be fun. You just lean on me and show up.*

After I finished writing the book, the Lord began to open all kinds of doors; I started speaking at events on weekends while still working at Mobil. During those five years I would say to the Lord, "I don't know if I can do this," and he would say, *I'm doing it through you. Just keep showing up.*

In 1995, I got a call from Steve Arterburn asking me if I would join Barbara Johnson, Marilyn Meberg, and Patsy Clairmont to speak at an event called Laughing Ladies. We declined—not the offer, but that name had to go. Steve could see that women needed more joy (his first instruction was "Make 'em laugh"), so we finally decided to call the event The Joyful Journey. That was the beginning of Women of Faith.

At the time, *nothing* like this was available for women. When we went to arenas and started doing events in the round, it created a different dynamic from what women had ever experienced. They could see each other, they could see us, we could see them, and God was watching over all of it, saying, *This is going to be fun. You just lean on me and show up.*

On that California highway all those years ago, all I could see was that I wasn't happy. Only God could see the big picture of what he had planned. He saw me on my way to a job I didn't think mattered, and he sees you wherever you are right now. More than that, he sees the plans he has for you. If you listen, I bet you'll hear him whisper in your heart, *This is going to be fun. You just lean on me and show up.*

Father, it's so comforting to know that you see my future as well as my present. When I get overwhelmed, help me remember that you will work through me as long as I lean on you and show up.

A Kiss from God

by Allison Allen

*I am confident I will see the LORD's goodness while I am
here in the land of the living.*

PSALM 27:13

Have you ever needed a kiss from God? You know
the kind I'm talking about—the intimate ges-
ture that lets us know we are seen and known. That
sweet, fatherly kiss on the forehead that reminds us
just whose we are. I think God delights in answering
those prayers.

Maybe you are going through a particularly rough
patch right now. Perhaps you just received some news
that your heart can't quite make room for. Or maybe
you've just moved to a new city and are living in a
house full of cardboard boxes and without a new friend
in sight. Maybe the company with the job you thought

was "in the bag" has just instituted a hiring freeze. Maybe your washing machine just broke. Maybe you're simply tired and can't fold one more basket of clothes. . . .

And maybe what you need more than anything else in the whole wide world is a kiss from your Father.

Psalm 27, penned by David, has one of my favorite verses in the whole of the Bible. "I am confident I will see the LORD's goodness while I am here in the land of the living" (verse 13). Even though the psalm sounds a note of triumphant faith, it also speaks of enemies, rejection, trouble, and the pain of false witness. As David wraps up his song, he proclaims that, even in the midst of the joy and tragedy that is life, he knows he will see signs of God's provision and presence *on this side of heaven.*

I suspect that our heavenly Father is often giving us tangible evidence of his nearness. Perhaps it is when we ask for intimacy, when we pray for a sign of his "goodness . . . in the land of the living," that our hearts are tuned to his kind overtures.

Several months ago, I had one of those days and,

hence, prayed one of those prayers. The prayer went something like, "Lord, could you please let me know you see?" I didn't even really know what I needed; I just knew that I was feeling a bit shaky and needed him. I remember going to a movie later with my husband, coming out, and finding a message on my phone from a pastor friend whom I hadn't spoken to in more than six months. Through many years, particularly in college, this wonderful gentleman had been a father figure to me and to many. I hit play, and then I heard his voice saying, "I just want to let you know how proud I am of you, and how well I think you're doing. Keep going."

It brought fresh tears to my eyes. It was exactly what I had needed but hadn't known to specifically ask for. God had just blown me a kiss, in a way that only God can.

Dear heavenly Father, help me to watch for the "kisses" you blow my way this week.

He Sees You, Too

by Jenna Lucado Bishop

*A woman in the crowd had suffered for twelve years with
constant bleeding. She had suffered a great deal from many
doctors, and over the years she had spent everything she
had to pay them, but she had gotten no better. In fact, she
had gotten worse. She had heard about Jesus, so she came
up behind him through the crowd and touched his robe. For
she thought to herself, "If I can just touch his robe, I will be
healed." Immediately the bleeding stopped, and she could feel
in her body that she had been healed of her terrible condition.*

MARK 5:25-29

This woman was ostracized. Legally, under the
Jewish Law (aka the Mosaic Law), she was considered unclean. This meant she couldn't touch her
family, go to synagogue, or hang out with friends. She
was alone, afraid, and hadn't been touched for twelve
years. Wow. Think about how old you were twelve

years ago. Now, imagine not having human contact for that long.

The woman, desperate for answers, with nothing left, finally turned to Jesus.

Her timid approach to Jesus, coming up behind him, points to a hurt deeper than her physical wound. It points to a shame that was hurting her heart. She didn't want to be seen physically, but her soul longed to be seen after years of no one touching her or acknowledging her. So she reached out to God who, little did she know, created her and had been with her every moment of every day. And on top of it all, what great faith she had! To believe that a light touch would cure her? That is true faith.

Amidst the crowd pushing him and shoving him, Jesus asked, "Who touched me?" Can you see how the disciples would have thought Jesus' question was a little crazy? Picture yourself in a crowded place. Maybe at the mall on Christmas Eve for a last-minute gift or fighting your way to the parking lot through the crowd that rushes the doors after the concert or game is over. Now imagine in the middle of the hustle and bustle, yelling, "Hey! Who touched me?" You may get some looks, some eye rolls, some laughs.

So why do you think Jesus asked this question? Was it because he really wanted to know who it was that touched him? Didn't Jesus know everything? Why do you think an all-knowing God, in the middle of a crowd, asked, "Who touched me?"

Jesus never asked a question to get an answer for himself. He always asked questions so that we could get an answer. But I can't help but wonder if Jesus asked the question to draw her out of her hiding place, to draw her out of shame, to give her attention, to let her know he saw her. See, her physical needs had been answered. But Jesus wanted to answer her deeper question, her deeper need: "Am I loved? Am I ever cared about or seen?"

Do you know that Jesus sees you?

—Love Is . . .

Father, thank you that even when I feel lost in a crowd, you see and care about me.

The Lord Looks at the Heart

by Christine Caine

*When they arrived, Samuel took one look at Eliab and
thought, "Surely this is the LORD's anointed!" But
the LORD said to Samuel, "Don't judge by his appearance
or height, for I have rejected him. The LORD doesn't see
things the way you see them. People judge by outward
appearance, but the LORD looks at the heart."*

1 SAMUEL 16:6-7

When the prophet Samuel saw Eliab, the eldest
son of Jesse, he assumed that Eliab was the one
chosen to be the next king of Israel based on his exter-
nal appearance. The only problem was that although
Eliab looked to be the best choice, he was not God's
first choice. So often we can make the same mistake.
We think if someone is talented or gifted or smart or
eloquent, he or she must be the one whom God has
chosen. More often than not we think everyone else is
a better choice than we would be.

God has always chosen those whom no one else

SUMMER

would choose so that his glory can shine through them. God sees possibility when no one else does. God sees potential when no one else does. God sees faithfulness when no one else does. God sees loyalty when no one else does.

God always sees more in us than we see in ourselves. He sees a king when everyone else sees a shepherd boy. If you feel overlooked or forgotten by man, know that God sees you. God has chosen and called you. Will you respond to that call today?

Have you ever felt that God could not use you because of your own limitations? Make a list of all of the strengths that God has given you and tell him you are ready to be used by him.

Father, I want to fulfill the calling you have placed on my life. I am ready to be used by you. Help me to not get in my own way.

He Knows My Name

by Mary Graham

I will give you treasures hidden in the darkness— secret riches. I will do this so you may know that I am the LORD, the God of Israel, the one who calls you by name.

ISAIAH 45:3

G et this: There is a dry cleaner in my neighborhood that I rarely frequent. In fact, I have been there maybe a dozen times. Total. I use another dry cleaner regularly, but on occasion, I need a drop-off and pickup in short order—so since it's on the route I take to work, I take something on the way in and pick it up on my trip home. I did that today.

Here's the amazing thing: The guy who works there knows my name! He never does any kind of paperwork or asks me anything. He just says, with a bit of an accent, as I hand my dirty laundry through the window, "Thank you, Ms. Graham." And although

I'm rarely speechless, I just stare at him without saying anything.

As I drive away, for at least five minutes I'm thinking, *He knows my name. How in the world does he know my name?* For the life of me, I cannot figure it out. We've never shared a sentence of conversation. I don't wear a name tag. I have absolutely no idea if he owns the place or manages it. I know only one thing about him: He knows my name.

Hmmm.

So today as I drove to work thinking about the mystery of this, it occurred to me that God—the God of the universe, the God of heaven and earth, the almighty, awesome, amazing God—knows my name. He knows me. He's numbered the hairs on my head (for whatever reason!). He created me and knows everything there is to know about me. He knows me, calls me by name, and loves me.

And he knows you, and he calls you by name, and no paperwork is required. By his Spirit and through the majesty of his grace, you are his. We are his people and the sheep of his pasture. "I am the good shepherd; I know my own sheep, and they know me" (John 10:14).

If I stand amazed that a total stranger remembers my name, how much more delighted and amazed can I be, knowing that the one who loves me most knows me best?

Lord, the fact that I am known to you and loved by you gives me so much hope. You are faithful to hear my prayers and attend to my needs. You are near to the brokenhearted and save those who are crushed in spirit. Your Word reminds me that you will come when I call and that if I draw near to you, you will draw near to me.

Where Are You?

by Marilyn Meberg

When the cool evening breezes were blowing, the man and his wife heard the LORD God walking about in the garden. So they hid from the LORD God among the trees. Then the LORD God called to the man, "Where are you?"

GENESIS 3:8-9

Let's do a quick replay of the post-apple scene in the garden. Because Adam and Even had eaten of the tree of the knowledge of good and evil, they knew they had done a "bad thing." Genesis 3:8-9 describes their shame: "Toward evening they heard the LORD God walking about in the garden, so they hid themselves among the trees. The LORD God called to Adam, 'Where are you?'"

The point here is not their hiding in shame; we all do that when we've done a bad thing. The point here is that *God came looking for them*; He sought them out with the question, "Where are you?"

God didn't ask the question because He didn't

21

know where they were. He asked the question that they might *admit* where they were. He also asked the question so they could choose to respond to Him—or try to avoid him by remaining hidden. They chose to come out of hiding.

When they did so, God did the most amazingly nurturing thing: "And the LORD God made clothing from animal skins for Adam and his wife" (v. 21). They had not known shame before they disobeyed, but having done so, they needed clothes.

God seeks us out, even when we've made bad choices. When we open ourselves to Him, when we share our darkest "secrets," He does not leave us to sink deeper and deeper into our chosen messes. Instead, He comes after us, shining his heavenly light on those secrets hiding in the dark corners of our hearts, and asking for our response to the question, "Where are you?" He does not ever sever the inseparable bonds He wraps around us.

There are times when God asks the question, "Where are you?" and, out of shame, you don't respond. You remain hidden. You keep your distress or your failures a secret, embarrassed by what you have done—or perhaps are still doing.

God wants us to feel safe enough to answer, to tell Him the "secrets" He already knows. Why? He wants to maintain our connection. He wants us to feel the inseparable bond that melds Him to us. He wants to assure us that He will work out His plans for our lives.

—*Tell Me Everything*

O Lord, I don't want to hide from you. Help me lift my eyes to you and feel your compassion and forgiveness. May your love and mercy flow over me and wash me clean from failures and sin. Today, I want to be closer to you and live my life in the shadow of your presence.

That's Redonkulous

by Korie Robertson

O LORD, you have examined my heart and know everything about me.

PSALM 139:1

Redonkulous is just a big, crazy, fun word that means "bigger than anything we can imagine." You could say our television show, *Duck Dynasty*, is a bit redonkulous. We used this word in the Vacation Bible School curriculum that we wrote to teach children that with God, absolutely anything is possible! When *Duck Dynasty* first came out, we thought the show was funny, and we laughed at ourselves like families do when they're watching home movies. But we had no idea if other people would laugh along with us. We certainly never dreamed we would end up with backpacks with the guys' faces on them, Willie Chia Pets, doormats, and even *Duck Dynasty* underwear. As a family, we're honored that so many people have found our show worthy of their time to watch, but I'll admit—it's a little strange, and, dare I say, *redonkulous* to see that happening.

One thing that has been interesting is that so many people think that because they see us on television they actually know us. I'll have people yell my name across a parking lot, or just walk up and give me a hug. At first I expected to look up and see someone I knew, but now I'm used to people *feeling* like they know me, even if we've never met. It's true that what you see on the show is pretty much what you get in real life, although our real life involves more normal things, like taking out the trash and going to school, practices, and church. When people see us around the table at the end of each *Duck Dynasty* episode, thanking God for our blessings and laughing together over the day's events, they get a good glimpse into who we are.

Most of the people we meet who watch our show are incredibly kind and a joy to meet, but being "known" by so many people means there are some who don't agree with how we are living our lives, and they think they have the right to weigh in on everything we do. I've had to talk to our kids about that. I tell them it doesn't matter what people who don't know us say or think. Even Jesus, who was perfect, was hated and criticized. He was called a glutton and a drunkard by people who did not know him or understand what he was about. Paying too much attention to people who don't even know you but love you, or to those who hate you, will either give you a big head or shoot your confidence right down the drain.

The fact that you know God—having a relationship with him and knowing how he feels about you—is all that really matters. God knows you. And I mean *really* knows you, as in "counting every hair on your head" knows you. Not just the "you" that's on public display, but the real you, the person you are when the cameras aren't rolling. And the best thing about it is that he loves you on the good days and the bad, whether you are in tune with his will or struggling with doubt. He loves you whether or not anyone else in the world knows you. God has examined your heart.

He knows everything about you, and still he loves you redonkulously.

Father, you know me better than anyone else. I am amazed (and grateful) that even though you know me so well, you love me so much. Thank you.

Dancing with Lazarus

by Ellen Miller

Jesus shouted, "Lazarus, come out!" And the dead man came out, his hands and feet bound in graveclothes, his face wrapped in a headcloth. Jesus told them, "Unwrap him and let him go!"

JOHN 11:43-44

Jesus decided to show Mary and Martha a whopper of a miracle: He raised Lazarus from the dead. Jesus said, "Lazarus, come out!" He then instructed the witnesses to "unwrap him and let him go!" Lazarus, bound head to toe in his funeral wrappings, was probably more than a bit anxious to get out of his gauze. (I can relate—you should see me stripping out of panty hose after an eight-hour sentence.)

This story contains numerous teachings and subplots that are pretty awesome (you can read all about it in John chapter 11), but it's the statement "Unwrap him and let him go" that speaks loudest to me. Not until my brush with a life-altering disease did I begin to understand God's desire to remove us from our bindings and free us from trappings of this world; free us from our negative self-talk; free us of our twisted thinking toward our families and fellow man.

Are you dead and wrapped up spiritually?

Are you dead and wrapped up emotionally?

Are you dead and wrapped up in your own self-oppression?

I can only imagine that Mary, Martha, and Lazarus had a pretty rich conversation around the dinner table that evening. Like me, I'm sure Lazarus saw his brief time on earth through new lenses too.

"So go ahead. Eat your food with joy, and drink your wine with a happy heart, for God approves of this!" (Ecclesiastes 9:7).

Once he was rehydrated, I bet ole Lazarus was dancing to beat the band! So with that, I have decided to dance in my new body too . . . the polka, the fox-trot, the rumba . . . it doesn't matter to me. I have a new perspective on the steps I'm to take.

—*The One Year Book of Inspiration for Girlfriends*

Dear Lord Jesus, we bring our broken hearts and burdens to you, knowing you can "unwrap and untangle" our lives when they get messy. Thank you that you have promised to help in times of trouble and that you are the voice behind us saying which way we should take. We cast our cares on you and receive your comfort. Work on our behalf, that others might know and see your great power and faithfulness.

Free to Not Fit In

by Anita Renfroe

Store your treasures in heaven, where moths and rust cannot destroy, and thieves do not break in and steal.

MATTHEW 6:20

I know that those of you who live in California are proud of your great state. It's got lots of interesting topography (deserts, oceans, mountains, lush valleys, redwoods, and national parks), but with it you also have your mudslides, wildfires, and those occasional tremors known as earthquakes. My husband, John, and I have enjoyed the times we've had to come out to LA. Every time we see the big buildings and the swaying palm trees, without fail, we feel like the characters from *The Beverly Hillbillies* coming to town. If we just had the old flatbed truck with Granny rockin' on top, our feeling would have an image to go along with it.

I used to love watching that show when I was a kid. I recall coming home when I was a fourth and fifth grader, grabbing a bowl of ice cream, turning on the TV, and watching (in syndicated succession) *Gilligan's Island*, *Get Smart*, and *The Beverly Hillbillies*.

The thing I loved about *The Beverly Hillbillies* is that the Clampetts were such the fish-out-of-water family (as were *The Addams Family* and *The Munsters*, now that I think about it). The characters had been dropped into an environment and a lifestyle that was foreign to them, and they were trying their best to understand the values and the customs of this strange place. Their misinterpretations and ways of adapting to these challenges were the stuff of sitcom hilarity, right down to "warsh-ing" their long underwear down in the "cement pond." And although Uncle Jed had struck oil and they were incredibly wealthy, they continued to live as though they had the same resources afforded them back in their home state.

At my core, I completely understand that mindset. There are so many times I am acutely aware that I don't fit in. The Bible tells us that we are sojourners in a strange land and that our Father owns it all. So—in essence—we *are The Beverly Hillbillies*. We won't ever completely fit into a worldview that says, "Get all you can get, because you only go around once!" and "Look out for number one!" Instead, we are part of an upside-down culture that says, "The greatest among you must be a servant" (Matthew 23:11) and "The last will be first" (Matthew 20:16) and "Whoever loses their life for me will find it" (Matthew 10:39, NIV).

If we are living these principles out every day, we will certainly be thought of as (at best) naive and (at worst) weird. But we are wealthy in ways that are not ostentatious. We have an embarrassment of riches in the things that money cannot buy: In joy, peace, and love, we are all billionaires.

Heavenly Father, I want to live my life in ways that are pleasing to you. Help me to have a heavenly perspective and a grateful heart. You have blessed me in so many ways; forgive me when I get so focused on only the things I don't have and forget to recognize all the great things you have done for me.

Exchanging Fear for Fearlessness

by Patsy Clairmont

I will give you peace in the land, and you will be able to sleep with no cause for fear.

LEVITICUS 26:6

In the New Testament we have the joy of listening in as the seeking, the lost, the broken, the forgotten, the paralyzed, and the skeptical gather around Jesus. The Lord, who understood their frayed and scattered conditions, prescribed truth, direction, wholeness, mercy, forgiveness, love, and liberty for all who came with an ear to hear and a heart to receive.

Interestingly, the ones who were the most receptive were the most obviously damaged (lepers, crippled, grief stricken, neglected). That confirms what I've always suspected: The things we fear (pain, failure, disgrace, rejection, limitations) are ultimately some of our finest teachers, educating us in compassion, grace, wisdom, and understanding.

I have great empathy for those who struggle with erratic emotions because I know how overwhelming unpredictable feelings can be, feelings that flood in with such force they affect even your physical well-being. In my emotionally chaotic years, I had more symptoms than a dog has fleas. But you can treat fleas, whereas neurotic symptoms only leave the doctor scratching his head and the patient feeling hopeless. My fear-based illness kept me living a restricted, suffocating lifestyle.

At first, in my agoraphobic years, I coddled my fearful feelings to protect myself. I was already in a relationship with Christ, but if I was to survive, I would have to trust him at new levels. I would have to face my fears.

Slowly, as I inched toward freedom, Christ assisted me in finding my lost and hidden emotions. Pearl by priceless pearl, he restrung my necklace. He taught me to trade in my panic for the pearl of peace, to switch my weakness for the pearl of his strength, and to exchange my fear for the pearl of his fearlessness.

I love the chorus, "Turn your eyes upon Jesus, look full in his wonderful face, and the things of earth will grow strangely dim in the light of his glory and grace."[1] And that, my friend, includes our fears. They will wither in his presence while we grow in grace.

During my healing trek, I learned I was priceless to him because of his boundless love for me. And that's how he feels about you! So, no matter how unstrung you feel, or how many pearls you've lost, he longs to gather you up in his arms and calm your every fear.

—*Boundless Love*

Lord, you did not give us a spirit of fear, but rather a spirit of power, love, and a sound mind. Today I relinquish my fears to you, I renounce feelings of insecurity and anxiety, and I receive a calm and stable spirit and will walk in the freedom you freely give. I put my trust in you.

A High-Profile Relationship

by Lisa Harper

He brought me to the banqueting house, and his banner over me was love.

SONG OF SOLOMON 2:4, NKJV

Chapter 1 [of the Song of Solomon] records the love language of Solomon and his would-be bride, Shulamith, in a private setting, a dark theater, if you will. But their sweet talk continues in the very public atmosphere of the banquet house in chapter 2. They've essentially gone from a clandestine booth in an off-the-beaten-path eatery to a mall—on the day after Thanksgiving. They're bound to run into tons of people they know. Friends and strangers are sure to see them holding hands. It's going to be obvious to *everyone* that they're dating.

And to make his sentiments perfectly clear, just

in case anyone missed the fact that they are making goo-goo eyes at each other and are wearing matching T-shirts, Solomon starts waving a big banner with "I love this woman" painted on it. This man's behavior declares, "I want everyone to know how much I love you, baby. I want to shout it from the rooftops!"

Like Solomon in this Love story, God doesn't attempt to conceal or disguise his affection for us. Scripture never records him being aloof in front of people after whispering sweet nothings in the dark. He doesn't try to act cool and jam his hands in his pockets when others see you in public together. God has been up front about his pursuit of us from the beginning of biblical history.

He advertised his bond with the Israelites via a supernatural blimp in the wilderness. It was a cloud by day and morphed into a ball of fire at night (Exodus 13:17-22). Not exactly subtle. And his death on a cross wasn't what you'd call understated, either. Remember what the men ask Jesus on the Emmaus Road?

Are you the only one in Jerusalem who hasn't heard what's happened during the last few days?

In other words, "Good night! Haven't you been watching CNN or reading the newspaper? Everybody's been talking about how this guy named Jesus was killed at Golgotha!" Our Messiah's death on the cross was a very public execution. His matchless valentine gift made headlines all over the ancient world.

God is not secretive about his love for us. He shouts his affections for us from the rooftop of the universe!

—*What Every Girl Wants*

Thank you, Father, that you make it so clear in your Word that you love me with a love that lasts forever. Help me to never forget that.

Looking through the Eyes of Love

by Sheila Walsh

When the accusers heard this, they slipped away one by one,
beginning with the oldest, until only Jesus was left in the
middle of the crowd with the woman. Then Jesus stood up
again and said to the woman, "Where are your accusers?
Didn't even one of them condemn you?" "No, Lord," she
said. And Jesus said, "Neither do I. Go and sin no more."

JOHN 8:9-11

*G*od, *do you see me here?*
Are you with me here?
I am frightened and alone.
God, can you love me here?
Can you reach me here?
I'm a million miles from home.

In 1992 I entered a prison to be set free. Even as I
type these words I see so clearly now that God often

takes us to the place of our greatest imprisonment to bring us his greatest deliverance.

I spent one month in that hospital. One month began to change my life and set me on a new path.

One month gave me a new compass for my journey. One month gave me a place and time to stop running and let God love me.

I wanted to be perfect, but in the place of my greatest imperfection I began to see through different eyes. I had tried for years to dress up the outer shell of my life, but when crumbled I could not escape that quiet voice in my heart.

I love you
I love you
I love you
I see you as you are and I love you
I always have
I always will
So I responded.

Nothing in my hands I bring
Simply to thy cross I cling[2]

I had nothing in common with the woman dragged before Jesus, and yet I had everything in common with her. We were lost, exposed, accused either externally or internally, and alone. Neither of us expected what we saw when we looked into the face of God. We both expected judgment and received mercy.

Perhaps if you stop for a moment you might hear this voice. Perhaps if you look up you, too, will be bowled over by a tidal wave of outrageous love if you will just let go of who you see yourself to be. Take another look through the eyes of God's outrageous love.

> *All to Jesus I surrender, Lord, I give myself to Thee;*
> *Fill me with Thy love and power, Let Thy blessing*
>   *fall on me.*
> *I surrender all, I surrender all,*
> *All to Thee, My blessed Savior,*
> *I surrender all.*[3]

—Outrageous Love

Thank you that you love me. Always. And forever.

My Father's Love

by Rhonda Bell

God is our merciful Father and the source of all comfort.

2 CORINTHIANS 1:3

O ne morning, I was alone in my room confessing (yet again) the sin I had walked into. I was really struggling and beaten down by the Accuser hurling my sin in my face, telling me the familiar lie that God could not, did not love me. I cried out to God for forgiveness and begged him to, in some way, show me he loved me that day. I needed visible, concrete assurance of his love. I got up from praying, and with all the activities of being a mother of four, I soon forgot my request and went about my day.

We were living in Lancaster, Pennsylvania, at the time, roughly a five-hour drive from my parents in

New Castle. In the afternoon, I was having a conversation with my oldest son when I heard the front door opening. When I turned to see who was entering the house, I was surprised to see my dad. Usually there would be phone calls and coordination before a visit. Not this time.

When I asked why he decided to visit, his reply was touching. He said, "I just woke up and was overwhelmed by the feeling that I needed to see you, so I jumped in the car." I enjoyed the day visiting with my dad.

It wasn't until later at night, when things were quiet, that God spoke to me and reminded me of the request I had made earlier. I hadn't made the connection: I had prayed but not watched for his reply.

I was overwhelmed by his love and answer to my cry. He did indeed love me—he had sent my earthly daddy to comfort me.

I thank God for his lavish display of love, prompting my father to visit and gently reminding me of his love. When my dad hugged me that day, it was my heavenly Father's arms that also held me.

*Heavenly Father, thank you for your precious love. Help me
to be mindful of all the "hugs" you send my way this week.*

$\left(\text{SUMMER}\right)$

This Is Not Quite What I'd Planned

by Stephen Arterburn

Now all glory to God, who is able, through his mighty power at work within us, to accomplish infinitely more than we might ask or think.

EPHESIANS 3:20

It was in 1995, in the midst of one of the most difficult seasons of my life, that I attended a seminar at what is now known as the Honda Center in Anaheim. I needed inspiration and encouragement because I had taken four (male) speakers on a twelve-city tour, and less than a thousand people had come to hear them. A mere thirty-five people had sat in a giant ballroom at the conference in Chicago. That was not quite what I had planned for my events.

That day in Anaheim, God laid on my heart the thought that no one had created a conference for women. Promise Keepers was booming while women who had kept their promises stayed home. My mission was to create an event designed simply to encourage women. (Ironically, I had produced smaller events in the early eighties to help women. God must have been preparing me for the creation of Women of Faith.)

I left that Anaheim seminar and called three women who were the best authors and speakers I knew: Barbara Johnson, Patsy Clairmont, and Luci Swindoll. They introduced me to another speaker, Marilyn Meberg. I told them of my past relationship disappointments and of my failure with the current conference—and in spite of it all they agreed to speak nine times in large churches in 1996.

I had been insensitive to women's needs and also witnessed some churches in which women served, but were not served. So I asked the speakers to talk about personal struggles and sorrows; to bring hope through God's truth; and to fill hearts with healing laughter. I even thought Laughing Ladies might be a great title . . . but through my failures I had learned to listen, and I heard from the speakers that they didn't think my title was so great. We eventually settled on the name "Women of Faith," but the first few years were all about joy; we crisscrossed the country with conferences titled A Joyful Journey, Bring Back the Joy, and Outrageous Joy—and then focused on a new theme each year that we prayed would resonate with women.

At the first conference, two thousand women filled the sanctuary, and three hundred watched the event on a giant television in the chapel. This instant success was not quite what I had planned, but it was what God had planned. I knew I must get out of the way. That first year, thirty-six thousand women attended. In 1997, attendance grew to more than one hundred and fifty thousand. When Women of Faith came to Anaheim, just two years after God had provided me with the vision for Women of Faith there, eighteen thousand women filled every seat and filled the arena with their glorious, healing laughter.

I didn't know what was needed, but God did. When we become part of what God has planned, it becomes much more than we could ever imagine or even expect.

Father, thank you that even when things don't go quite the way I had planned, your plan is always for my good. Help me to make my plan your plan.

God Sees

by Nicole Johnson

*When you give to someone in need, don't let your left hand
know what your right hand is doing. Give your gifts
in private, and your Father, who sees everything, will
reward you.*

MATTHEW 6:3-4

Were you ever asked to keep a secret as a child?
If it was a good secret, you might remember the way it glowed inside you, so much that you thought you might burst if you didn't tell. Or if it was a bad secret, the pain burned and burrowed deeper and deeper into your soul, growing into an ache you feared would never go away.

Things hidden inside us have a lot of power over us. Bad secrets can control us and shape us in negative ways. Some psychologists even go so far as to say that we are only as sick as our secrets, meaning the things that we keep hidden have a certain power over us. But when a negative secret is told or given the light of day, its power often evaporates. The deep, dark secret that our heart fears at 2 a.m. often seems foolish in the morning, or when we tell someone else what we have been afraid of.

Why don't we bring more dark secrets into the light? Sadly, we tuck them away and give them a place to increase, causing doubt, fear, and anxiety. To make matters worse, we cast our good deeds out in the open. We want people to know the positive things we do, believing this will encourage them and perhaps ourselves. Unfortunately, when we proudly tell others about our altruistic actions, just the opposite occurs, and often the power of the good disappears into the air around us.

So what if we turned this tendency upside down? What if we brought our dark deeds into the light, and took our good deeds into the deepest parts of our hearts? This is what Scripture tells us to do.

When you give a gift, don't sound a trumpet so everyone knows what you're doing. . . . Instead, give in secret, in a way no one knows. *Then, trust that your Father in heaven sees* (see Matthew 6:2-4).

Anything kept in secret has power, so don't waste this power on your bad deeds; instead, use it to multiply your good deeds! Give gifts in secret, and see how the goodness of these deeds will grow inside you, making you stronger, flooding your heart with goodness and light. And then regularly confess your wrongs. When you do, you will find the shame and guilt evaporating in the wind of forgiveness. Over time, this will change your heart and your character, making you more confident in who you really are on the inside.

Blessings on your week as you serve God in secret!

Heavenly Father, you know all my secrets. Give me wisdom to know what needs to be brought into the light and what should be kept just between us.

A Tale of Two Women

by Mary Graham

"I know the plans I have for you," says the LORD. "They are plans for good and not for disaster, to give you a future and a hope."

JEREMIAH 29:11

It all started with a desperate prayer. Wosene was hungry, distraught, and soaking wet. The tiny hut that housed her family was almost worthless when the rains came. Wosene felt unable to provide adequate shelter or food for her children. On her knees in her mud-filled home, she prayed for God to end her life. But God had other plans.

About that time, Donna Galli attended a Women of Faith event and learned about child sponsorship through World Vision. She heard how her monthly gift could provide a child somewhere in the world with clean water, nutritious food, health care, education, and spiritual nurture.

"I thought," Donna says, *"I can't do a lot, but I can probably do this."* At the World Vision table, Donna found the picture of a little girl with eyes that made her own fill with tears. "There was just absolutely no hope in this little girl's eyes."

The little girl she sponsored that day was Senayit, Wosene's oldest daughter. Donna wrote her a letter and soon got a response: "My family was about to be scattered when you started sponsoring us." With the help of translators, the letters flew back and forth. When Donna learned more about how difficult things were for Senayit and her family, she and her husband decided to sponsor Senayit's younger sister, and later the baby of the family, a little boy.

In addition to writing to the three sponsored children and their siblings, Donna began to correspond with Wosene. She mentored her, encouraged her, and reminded her that she was doing the best she could for her children. Two women connected over the miles, treasuring the letters and pictures that passed between them. The relationship deepened and grew more precious with each passing year. *I may never see them,* Donna thought, *but they see the same moon I see, the same sun I see . . . and they worship the same Lord that I worship. We are connected.*

When Donna was given the opportunity to travel to Ethiopia and meet her World Vision family, she couldn't pass it up. After nearly eight years of loving a family through letters and prayer, Donna and her husband, Jeff, found themselves in Wosene's world and in her arms. All the pictures sent through the mail had finally come to life.

I had the privilege of tagging along on that trip and was there when Wosene took Donna to the old hut with holes in the roof, where she had once prayed to end her life. Back then she didn't realize that God saw her need . . . and at the same time, he saw a woman on the other side of the planet . . . and he would bring them together to change both their lives.

No matter where you may be—in a leaky mud hut or in a crowded arena—he sees you, too. Who can tell what he has planned for you?

Father, thank you that no matter where I am, you are there with me.

Finding Pennies

by Shauna Niequist

I praise your name for your unfailing love and faithfulness;
for your promises are backed by all the honor of your name.

PSALM 138:2

Before I started collecting pennies, I used to throw them away, along with gum wrappers and used Kleenex. No one accepts them anymore, really. I keep hearing that they're going to take them out of circulation. Bank tellers glare at me when I try to hand them several hundred and ask for dollars and quarters instead. The man at the Mexican restaurant where I eat doesn't want them. I get the same thing every time. It always comes to $6.04. Six-oh-four. I hand him six or a ten or a twenty and then dig in my pockets for the pennies, but he shakes his head. No pennies, no.

All of a sudden, the loss of these pennies seemed tragic to me. So I started collecting them, in a pale blue bowl that my cousin Georgia gave me for Christmas. I sort them out of the more substantial silver coins in my pocket and set them in their new place, the smooth blue bowl. I don't know what I will do with them, but there is something satisfying about watching their numbers grow, a little army of copper coins.

My friend goes to a spiritual director, and I was asking her about it, and she said, basically, Sister Carmen asks her to talk about her life, and she points out the presence and action and grace of God when my friend didn't even notice it was there. So it was there all along, and the trick is learning to see it.

Each one of our lives is shot through, threaded in and out with God's provision, his grace, his protection, but on the average day, we notice it about as much as we really notice gravity or the hole in the ozone. So what I'm trying to do is learn to see the way Sister Carmen sees. Because once you start seeing the faithfulness and the hope, you see it everywhere, like pennies. And little by little, here and there, you realize that all of life is littered with bright copper coins, that all of life is woven with bits and stories of God's goodness.

When I look back now, with these new eyes, it's like there's a bright copper path I was walking on and didn't even know it. And it's the handful of pennies that I'm clutching in my sweaty hand that gives me the faith and the strength to move forward. What gives me hope is the belief that God will be faithful, because he has been faithful before, to me and the people around me. I need the reminders. I need to be told that he was faithful then, and then, and then. Just because I have forgotten how to see doesn't mean it isn't there. His goodness is there. His promises have been kept. All I need to do is see.

—*Cold Tangerines*

Father, open my eyes and help me see your faithfulness.

Faithful . . . Always

by Robin Johnson

*He comforts us in all our troubles so that we can
comfort others. When they are troubled, we will be able to
give them the same comfort God has given us.*

2 CORINTHIANS 1:4

The morning I received the call that my oldest
child was in the hospital, I didn't realize that I
was being held up by strong arms. God had things for
me to do, and so he filled me with his peace and presence, without my even realizing it. When the shocking
news of my son's death came, God strengthened me
in my need.

The day after the death of my son, my car broke
down in a grocery store parking lot and wouldn't start
again. At this point, though I had tried to have faith
through the ordeal, I glanced up at the sky and said,
"Really, God? You couldn't have given me just a bit

more grace, knowing what I have just gone through?" I felt what seemed like a gentle hug to my soul, and I admitted, "Okay, God . . . I know that you will never waste a moment. Even in this, you have a plan."

The tow truck driver seemed to sense that he could confide in me. He shared, in frustration, "My sister is dying of cancer . . . and it's killing me." I glanced over at him and said softly, "You know . . . if you had shared this with me the day before yesterday, I might not have understood how you felt, but . . . my son died yesterday morning. Now I think I have a better idea of what you are going through." At this point I had his full attention. His heart was ready to receive anything God might say.

I said to him, with the conviction that God was placing on my heart, "When my car broke down in the parking lot, I could have tried my best to get it to the shop by myself. But I couldn't have done it. It is way too heavy for me." As we pulled up to the repair shop, I said, "I needed your help to get it here." The man who had opened his heart up to me was listening, so I added, "You and I have a burden that is way too heavy for us to carry on our own. We simply can't do it. We need God's help to carry so much pain." I then promised him, "If you will reach out to God, he'll hear you . . . he'll respond."

The tow truck driver looked over at me, saying, "I think I'll be considering your words."

Through the death of my son I learned that the Lord is willing to meet us in our need, even before we realize that we are in need. He may use us to bless others, even in the midst of our own pain. He is faithful . . . always.

Lord, fill us this day with your peace, and may your presence sustain and strengthen us through difficult days. Help us never lose sight of the hurt in others, and help us to comfort them with the comfort we ourselves have received from you. Thank you for your providence and that our pain can be used for our progress.

Your Destiny

by Max Lucado

You didn't choose me. I chose you.

JOHN 15:16

You are God's child. He saw you, picked you, and placed you. "You did not choose me; I chose you" (John 15:16, NCV). Before you are a butcher, baker, or cabinetmaker, male or female, Asian or black, you are God's child. Replacement or fill-in? Hardly. You are his first choice.

Such isn't always the case in life. Once, just minutes before I officiated a wedding, the groom leaned over to me and said, "You weren't my first choice."

"I wasn't?"

"No, the preacher I wanted couldn't make it."

"Oh."

"But thanks for filling in."

"Sure. Anytime." I considered signing the marriage license "Substitute."

You'll never hear such words from God. He chose you. The choice wasn't obligatory, required, compulsory, forced, or compelled. He selected you because he wanted to. You are his open, willful, voluntary choice. He walked onto the auction block where you stood, and he proclaimed, "This child is mine." And he bought you "with the precious blood of Christ, as of a lamb without blemish and without spot" (1 Peter 1:19, NKJV). You are God's child.

You are his child forever.

Don't believe the tombstone. You are more than a dash between two dates. "When this tent we live in— our body here on earth—is torn down, God will have a house in heaven for us to live in, a home he himself has made, which will last forever" (2 Corinthians 5:1, GNT). Don't get sucked into short-term thinking. Your struggles will not last forever, but you will.

God will have his Eden. He is creating a garden in which Adams and Eves will share in his likeness and love, at peace with each other, animals, and nature. We will rule with him over lands, cities, and nations. "If we endure, we shall also reign with Him" (2 Timothy 2:12, NKJV).

Believe this. Clutch it. Tattoo it on the interior of your heart. It may seem that the calamity sucked your life out to sea, but it hasn't. You still have your destiny.

—*You'll Get Through This*

Heavenly Father, the fact that you *have chosen* me *is more than I can fully comprehend. I pray I will never forget it. You are my Savior, Redeemer, Deliverer, Counselor, Provider, and Healer; I praise you for who you are. I surrender all the details of my life to you. In all my ways I will acknowledge you and ask you to direct my path.*

He Knows What We're Made For

by Jen Hatmaker

Since we are surrounded by such a huge crowd of witnesses
to the life of faith, let us strip off every weight that slows
us down, especially the sin that so easily trips us up. And let
us run with endurance the race God has set before us.

HEBREWS 12:1

God made us all as an entire package. It all counts. There are no throwaway qualities. In fact, those might help point you in just the right direction. Nothing is wasted: not a characteristic, a preference, an experience, a tragedy, a quirk. *Nothing.* It is all you, and it is all purposed, and it can all be used for great and glorious good.

Maybe your best thing won't draw a paycheck, but it is still where you shine and glow and come to life and bless the world. May I legitimize your gifts, please? Just because you don't get a pay stub doesn't mean you should shrink back or play small or give it all up. Do your thing. Play your note. We are all watching, learning, moved. You are making the world kinder, more beautiful, wiser, funnier, richer, better. Give your gifts the same attention and space and devotion you would if you were paid. (Or paid *well*. Some of us do our best, most meaningful work for peanuts. Do not be shamed out of your race for a bigger paycheck. I did not make a living as a writer for *years*. When I once told my neighbor I was a Christian author, she exclaimed: "Oh! Is there a market for that?" Me: "I have no idea.")

Run your race.

Maybe you need to invest in your gifts. Take a class. Go to a conference. Sign up for a seminar. Start that small business. Put that website up. Build in some space. Say yes to that project. Work with a mentor. Stop minimizing what you are good at and instead throw yourself into it with no apologies. Do you know who is going to do this for you? *No one*. You are it. Don't bury that talent, because at the end of the day, the only thing your fear will net you is one buried talent in a shallow grave.

How many of us are trotting out that tired cliché—"I'm waiting for God to open a door"—and He is all "I love you, but get going, Precious Snowflake, because most of the time chasing the dream I put in your heart looks surprisingly like hard work. Don't just stand there; bust a move." (God often sounds like Young MC.) You are good at something for a reason. God designed you this way; this is on purpose. It isn't fake or a fluke or small. These are the mind and heart and hands and voice you've been given: *Use them.*

Let the rest of us grin at you while you run your race. Let us be proud. Let us be inspired and grateful that God made you to do this thing and you are doing it *like a boss.* The timing is never right. Forget that. It won't just fall into your lap. That's fake. You are probably not guaranteed success. Sorry. This might be a crapshoot. It will be hard and require sacrifices, not just from you, but maybe from your people, and you might step out on shaky, shaky legs. But off you go because you were not created to stand still, even though that is safe and familiar and you are practically guaranteed never to fall or stumble or grow weary.

We were made to run.

Run.

Heavenly Father, strengthen me today to run faster and harder and give all I've got to accomplish my purpose in this life. Give me the heart of a champion, and may I be stronger and braver than in years past. I will not shrink back, but I will press on even through obstacles and adversities . . . and I will be courageous!

I Want to Be Like Them

by Mary Graham

If the Son sets you free, you are truly free.

JOHN 8:36

One day I was racing through a local store when I heard someone saying, "Is it you? Is it really you?" I turned to look for someone famous walking by . . . but I was stunned to see the person being spotted was *me.*

The "spotter's" name was Sunny. She worked at the makeup counter, and she had a story to tell. "The first year I came to Women of Faith, my daughter-in-law was leaving my son." Just before the Dallas event that year, Sunny's daughter-in-law announced she was leaving her husband and their children to become an exotic dancer.

"I asked her to go to the Women of Faith event before she made such a huge decision," Sunny remembered. Surprisingly, the young woman agreed. The two of them showed up at the arena on a Friday night. They sang, laughed, listened, and entered into the experience. Watching the women on stage and in the audience, Sunny's daughter-in-law turned to her and exclaimed, "I want to be like them! How can I be like them?"

"It was," Sunny said, "life-changing." As a result of her Women of Faith experience, Sunny's daughter-in-law did *not* leave her family (nor did she become an exotic dancer). That weekend her life was changed, and now, a dozen or more years later, she's never been the same. Sunny told me, "Women of Faith started a process in her life that God was faithful to finish. And today she loves the Lord, and my grandkids are being raised in the Lord. How awesome is that?"

Since then, Sunny and her daughter-in-law have brought literally hundreds of women with them to Women of Faith events. "Every year," Sunny says, she loves "watching God change lives and watching him meet someone who is devastated with things that have happened."

Just think of all the women who have been set free because, at a difficult time in both of their lives, one woman reached out to another. That so inspires me. "You know," Sunny said, "he uses ordinary people, and all he needs is for you to be willing." This week, I'm determined to be willing and available to be used by God. Will you join me? Who knows what he may choose to do through us!

Lord, I want to be used by you and to cooperate with your plan for my life. I pray today you'd bring someone across my path whom I can encourage and bless. Don't let me get so caught up in my own life and "to-do list" that I miss divine appointments you have orchestrated.

Tempted to Worry?
Fahgeddaboudit

by Luci Swindoll

Don't worry about anything; instead, pray about everything.
Tell God what you need, and thank him for all he has done.

PHILIPPIANS 4:6

I was walking through the Museum of Modern Art in New York, trying to get to all six floors in one afternoon. I had to move pretty fast in front of those great paintings that I love so much. Suddenly, something stopped me dead in my tracks. It was a framed piece of vellum with a throwaway comment penciled in the center. In just six lines, Jenny Holzer, an American conceptual artist, captured a nagging feeling that I could completely identify with—the sense that even when there is no obvious reason to fear, something is brewing behind the scenes, and "there will be trouble."[4]

The artist's words amused me because they capture

in a nutshell how each of us often feels. So I decided to hang around a few minutes and watch people's reactions to this piece of art. First of all, *everybody* stopped. Second, *everybody* laughed. And third, *everybody* commented. Mostly it was, "Oh my goodness. I can't tell you how often I've felt that. How did this Jenny Holzer know?" or, "Look, honey . . . it's like a page from my diary."

But it was a dialogue between two New Yorkers that I enjoyed the most. It gave me pause. One woman said, "That's me. *Absolutely me.* The first thing I do every morning is worry." Then her companion said (in his strong Brooklyn brogue), "Ah've told ya not to worry. Why ya worry when ahm wid'cha?" They never took their eyes off the picture, as if it could harbor or analyze their personal confessions.

I love it when something reflects the human condition in such a unique way. That couple could have been any of us. We worry about general things in preparation for the trouble we know will come soon. It's the suspicion upon which we build a case for concern. And all the while God is saying, *Why ya worry when ahm wid'cha*? I'm trying to take him at his word, remembering that even if there do happen to be forces conspiring against me, he's bigger than they are and able to take care of everything that comes my way. The same is true for you. Relax.

I tried to find a reproduction of Jenny Holzer's words on a museum postcard so I could put them in my journal, but they didn't have one. That's okay. I've written them down so I don't forget them. And to the right I jotted, *Why ya worry when ahm wid'cha*? Now I'm thinking of hanging the whole thing on my own little museum wall. It's too good and too true to tuck away. And next time you're tempted to worry? Fahgeddaboudit.

Hang loose, my friends. God's got us covered on all sides.

Heavenly Father, I relinquish worry, stress, and undue concern over matters of which I have no control. I receive instead your peace and assurance that you are with me and have control over everything that touches my life. Create in me a calm and quiet spirit so that my heart and mind will be at peace.

A Cup of Freedom

by Marilyn Meberg

A cheerful heart is good medicine.

PROVERBS 17:22

When my husband, Ken, and I moved into our first little house, we were so taken by the darling garden that came with it that we decided to hold a garden party. One of the features of our new little garden was a not-so-little mint plant. I decided the perfect refreshment at a garden party on a warm California day would be mint tea, which I would make from scratch from the mint in our garden. What could possibly go wrong?

In order for you to have the full picture, you should know that my mother-in-law was not only a fabulous cook, but she also actually *wrote cookbooks*. Naturally, I felt that I had to live up to her high standards, which

I was certain I would do with this amazing mint tea concoction. I could just picture myself out in the garden, cup in hand, casually tossing out comments like "Oh, the tea? I made it myself with the mint from our garden. Would you like another cup?"

What with all the planning and preparations for what I fully expected to be the social event of the season, I didn't get around to making the tea until the morning of the party. I followed the recipe exactly . . . but the result was disappointing. I pictured mint tea as a vibrant shade of green, matching the leaves from whence it came. What I had was something significantly less interesting. *No matter*, I thought, *I'll just add a little more mint.* However, a little more did not have the desired effect, so I added a little *more* mint, then a little more and then a lot more, until finally, it was exactly the color I wanted.

All that extra minting took more time than I had anticipated, so there wasn't time to taste it. I proudly bore my beautiful beverage out to the garden and served a cup to my loving husband.

He promptly spat it out.

My dear friend Luci Swindoll says to take everything as a compliment, but Ken's reaction to my culinary masterpiece didn't seem particularly complimentary. So I tried the tea myself . . . and promptly spat it out. It was completely undrinkable. I was horrified. "What are we going to do? The guests will be here any minute!"

"Here's what we're going to do," Ken said. "When people arrive, we're going to say 'Would you like a cup of mint tea?' and then we're going to hand them one . . . and stand back."

And that's what we did.

The ability to appreciate the humor of a situation is a gift God has bestowed upon each of us, but it's a gift that is frequently unused because we take ourselves too seriously. Knowing who we are in Christ frees us to laugh, secure in the knowledge that even when we do something foolish, we are still loved by our Savior.

Father, your Word says that laughter is good medicine, and I am thankful for the relief and refreshment it brings my spirit and soul. Help me not to take myself too seriously and to calm down so I can enjoy some of the lighter days you have brought into my life . . . for my own benefit.

You Are God's Favorite

by Babbie Mason

Never be ashamed to tell others about our Lord.

2 TIMOTHY 1:8

You are God's favorite. He loves you as if you were an only child. You are His very own. Let me ask you this: What do you call the people who occupied the land of Canaan? The Canaanites, right? What do you call those who inhabited the land of Moab? The Moabites, yes? And what do you call the people who lived in the land of Israel? The Israelites, correct? Because you are a recipient of God's great love, because you occupy the land of His wonderful favor, what are you called? You are called a favorite!

When you realize how much you are loved by God, you become so filled up with His love and compassion that you want to share His love with others in your ordinary "walking-around" life. I don't know much, but one thing I do know for sure: God loves you as if you were the only one to love. He loves you just as much as He loves His own Son.

Do you believe that to the extent that you want to live it out? When you do, you can risk loving others to put love on the line. I've asked God to use me like that: however He wants and whenever He wants. One day He took me up on it. That day I was at the doctor's office to get my annual mammogram, and I was a bit anxious. Getting a mammogram is not one of my favorite things to do. The whole ordeal is uncomfortable, beginning with the gown the technician had given me to put on (which was less like a cotton gown and more like an oversized paper towel). And there's nothing I love better than having my teacups squeezed into saucers, if you know what I mean. But on an annual basis, I do what must be done.

I was waiting when I heard a soft knock at the door. Another nurse poked her head into the room. She had a smile on her face and a certain look in her eyes. She said, "Are you Babbie Mason?"

I sheepishly answered, "Uh . . . yeah?" She exclaimed with delight: "I knew it! I knew that was you! I saw you at a Women of Faith Conference! Would you mind singing my favorite song, 'Standing in the Gap'?"

She was asking for my permission while calling other nurses into the room. Quickly, I literally tried to pull it together. I adjusted the paper towel gown around me a little more, as if it had more to give. (It had nothing more to give.) But I was about to give the concert of a lifetime. The room filled with nurses, technicians, and only the Lord knows who else. Without so much as an apology, I opened my mouth and sang to encourage the hearts of women along life's journey.

I looked into each face as I sang. An examining room became holy ground, and a paper towel gown became a choir robe. I learned that day that people everywhere are starved for love. They don't care what the setting looks like. If there's a fire in your heart, they will draw near it to keep warm.

—*This I Know For Sure*

*Heavenly Father, may I always have a song in my heart
and a smile on my face to share with others. Even if
I don't have the gift of singing, I want to use my gifts to
bring you glory and to be a blessing to others. Increase
my passion and put a fire in my heart for ministry.*

God's Garden

by Allison Allen

*Yes, I am the vine; you are the branches. Those who remain
in me, and I in them, will produce much fruit. For apart
from me you can do nothing.*

JOHN 15:5

There is nothing yuckier in all the world than a
rotten tomato. If you've ever tried to pick one
from the vine or take one out of the veggie drawer
in your fridge, only to have it mush in your hand, you
know what I'm talking about. It's just plain gross—
definitely good for nothing other than the trash bin.

Less-than-perfect tomatoes have been used through
the ages to show the disdain of unimpressed audi-
ences for unlucky performers, to shame criminals, and
to pelt and punish those society deemed as "outcasts."
In our modern age, there are "rotten tomato" awards

and websites for those movies or performers who don't quite make the grade. Poor tomatoes! When they are perfectly ripe, they are one of the most-used ingredients in our culinary palette—pasta and pizza sauce, salad toppings, the ubiquitous ketchup. Oh, but let them turn the least bit bad, and out they go—fast. Or worse, they become a universal symbol for all that is deeply undesirable.

This is why you might have watched, with something akin to curiosity, as I painstakingly carved the not-so-great spots out of five smallish, certainly unimpressive tomatoes. With the precision of a surgeon, I cut out soft and mushy bits, keeping what was left of a perfectly good (and tasty!) fruit. I then promptly fed the tomatoes to my family for dinner. Why in the world would I bother? Why not grab other tomatoes that were pristine, or skip the process altogether? There is only one answer: I grew them.

Our church launched a community garden this year, and I was all in: turning the soil; weeding the Bermuda grass; organically fertilizing the zucchini, cucumbers, butternut squash, carrots, lettuce, and the oh-so-finicky tomatoes. No one using our garden had much luck with tomatoes, but I was determined to nurture them and get those vines to produce some fruit. So when they finally did, I was thrilled—even though the fruit wasn't perfect—and more than a little willing to stand at my kitchen sink, whittling said tomatoes down to half of their original size, just to get to the good parts. I was proud of those tomatoes.

I think Jesus feels the same way about us. I believe he watches over our gardens and cultivates them, even when the fruit we produce is less than perfect. If there is anything good or promising, he carefully tends to us, pruning us, knowing that with his care and oversight, we will produce good fruit. Check out Isaiah 27:2-3 and 65:8, as well as John 15, for just a few examples of God's care.

Why should he go to such trouble? Simple. He grew us. He loves us. And he is simply the best gardener around.

Father, help me to not dread the pruning process in my life, but to realize that you prune me to produce more in me. I want to grow in my relationship with you and bring forth good and useful fruit in my life. Thank you for nurturing and loving me.

The Immeasurable Love of God

by Patsy Clairmont

I have told you all this so that you may have peace in me.
Here on earth you will have many trials and sorrows. But
take heart, because I have overcome the world.

JOHN 16:33

For years, I kept thinking if God loved me he would rescue me out of my difficulties. There have *been* those times, but often he doesn't. I have been left to wade through high waters in low boots, which caused me to puzzle over God's love and scramble about to figure out faith.

Then as I delved deeper, which is one of the benefits of hardship, I realized that God tells us again and again in Scripture that . . . "in the world [we] will have tribulation" (John 16:33, NKJV).

Quite honestly, I just didn't want to believe it. I want life to be easier not only for me but for all those whom I love. Yet I have observed that change seldom occurs without struggle, whether it's a caterpillar wiggling free of his cocoon to fly or a person squiggling free of addiction to rise with newfound liberty.

Look in the Old Testament at Joseph's life—rejection, harassment, and injustice. And what was the result? A wise man came forth out of the prison, one who rose up to handle the responsibility of being second in command over the most powerful nation in the world at that time. Somehow Joseph was able to trust God's love regardless of being locked in a cell for an offense he didn't commit.

When I have to sit long in a doctor's waiting cell—I mean, office—I get whiny. I can't imagine Joseph's years in a dank, creepy room without peanut butter or Nick at Nite.

I have to remind myself when times crowd in with pressure, when people hurt my feelings, when my job loses its appeal, when my children fail to heed my advice, and when the newspapers read like doomsday reports, that God didn't promise life would be easy but that he would be with us as Buzz Lightyear (children's hero) would say, "To infinity and beyond!"

God can take a jail sentence and use it for the good of the prisoner, whether we are incarcerated behind iron bars or emotional ones. He uses our rejection issues to tutor us in the importance of compassion and inclusion. And harassment is just the right material to teach us the importance of knowing who we are in Christ, so we are not intimidated or persuaded that we are hopeless.

Try as we might, we cannot fully comprehend the immeasurable love of God—although one of the indicators is Jesus.

—*Infinite Grace*

Father, only your peace is perfect peace. Thank you that in times of greatest need, you comfort us with such peace.

$$\left(\text{AUTUMN} \right)$$

This Is *Big*

by Mary Graham

Now all glory to God, who is able, through his mighty power at work within us, to accomplish infinitely more than we might ask or think.

EPHESIANS 3:20

I learned about Women of Faith from Luci Swindoll, who called after one of the first events back in 1996 to tell me, "Mary, this is gonna be *big*!" I didn't believe her. I thought it was probably a nice enough event, but "big"? Surely not.

It wasn't long before I began volunteering as the emcee for events on the weekends. Meanwhile, I was working full-time at Campus Crusade for Christ (now known as Cru) for my "day job." One day Bill Bright, the founder of Campus Crusade, called and asked if I would meet with him. Luci was staying at my house at the time, so I brought her along. Bill graciously asked Luci how and what she was doing, so she told him all about Women of Faith.

"Who presents the gospel at that event?" Bill asked.

"No one," Luci replied. "They're all Christians."

Bill asked how many were coming, and Luci said, "Fifteen thousand."

"Luci," Bill gently said, "if there are fifteen thousand people coming to the event, they are not *all* Christians." Then he told her, "Mary will go, and she'll share the gospel."

I already had something like fifteen jobs (at least, it felt that way), so I wasn't sure I needed one more, but in the end, that's what happened. We started presenting a simple gospel message at each event, inviting women to put their faith in Jesus. We even shut down the bookstore booths on the concourse during that time so there wouldn't be any distractions. Then we started asking the people who had made a decision to mark a card and turn it in so we could send them some follow-up materials.

We had taken it for granted that women coming to a Christian women's event were all Christians, but the number of marked cards we received showed how wrong we were. It's so easy to assume that someone who appears to be okay and does the "right" things (like going to Women of Faith) already has a relationship with Jesus. But you never really know unless you ask.

After every event, the one thing everyone really wants to know is "How many decisions?" And not just the speakers; the entire staff at the arena and back at the office eagerly await the results. We focus on the number because we know that each digit represents a soul set free by God's love and grace.

The last time I checked, that number was just short of four *hundred* thousand. Luci was right all those years ago: This is *big*.

—————

Father, thank you that you do more than we could ever ask or think . . . like dying for us so that we could be set free.

Seeing the Messiah

by Thelma Wells

Anna, a prophet, was also there in the Temple. She was the
daughter of Phanuel from the tribe of Asher, and she was
very old. Her husband died when they had been married
only seven years. Then she lived as a widow to the age of
eighty-four. She never left the Temple but stayed there day
and night, worshiping God with fasting and prayer. She
came along just as Simeon was talking with Mary and
Joseph, and she began praising God. She talked about the
child to everyone who had been waiting expectantly for God
to rescue Jerusalem.

LUKE 2:36-38

Granny was a quiet, humble woman barely known
beyond our little back-alley neighborhood. Yet
her influence had a profound effect on me, and I've
tried my best to carry her character—and her faith—
with me wherever I've gone throughout the world.

Anna reminds me of Granny because she, too,
was very wise. What she knew was nothing short

of miraculous. She knew exactly who Jesus was long before other members of that community—and the world—discovered the Messiah in their midst. Anna's "insider knowledge" reminds me so much of Granny. She knew Jesus like nobody else, and she saw Jesus in the unlikeliest of people.

When Mary and Joseph brought the baby Jesus to the temple to be consecrated, they were first seen by a devout man named Simeon who'd been told by God that he would not die until he had seen the Messiah. Simeon was drawn to the temple courtyard the day Mary and Joseph brought Jesus there, and when he saw the baby, he cried out, "You may now dismiss your servant in peace. For my eyes have seen your salvation" (Luke 2:29-30, NIV).

Jesus's parents were amazed at Simeon's words, and then, as if to underscore what had happened, Anna appeared next on the scene. Luke 2:36-38 describes what happened: "There was also a prophetess, Anna. . . . She was very old; she had lived with her husband seven years after her marriage, and then was a widow until she was eighty-four. She never left the temple but worshiped night and day, fasting and praying. Coming up to them at that very moment, she gave thanks to God and spoke about the child to all who were looking forward to the redemption of Jerusalem" (NIV).

Anna could see the Messiah in that sweet baby's face, and she told others what she had seen. Granny did the same. She could see Jesus in people others might have turned away from. When someone created a poor impression or was unpleasant to be around, Granny would say, "You've gotta look *through* 'em to see Jesus, girl." Somehow, Granny had a way of seeing people's true heart—even when their behavior made you wonder if they had one!

Just as Anna somehow knew that the Messiah was being carried into the temple that day as a helpless infant, I try to see God's promises lived out in the world around me, as I do my best to live it out as well.

—*What These Girls Knew*

Heavenly Father, open my eyes that I may see you in those around me.

Seen as Who We Are

by Lisa Whelchel

*Our actions will show that we belong to the truth, so we
will be confident when we stand before God. Even if we
feel guilty, God is greater than our feelings, and he knows
everything. Dear friends, if we don't feel guilty, we can come
to God with bold confidence. And we will receive from him
whatever we ask because we obey him and do the things that
please him. And this is his commandment: We must believe in
the name of his Son, Jesus Christ, and love one another, just
as he commanded us. Those who obey God's commandments
remain in fellowship with him, and he with them. And we
know he lives in us because the Spirit he gave us lives in us.*

1 JOHN 3:19-24

When people think we are perfect, without insecurities or faults, it works against connection.
Vulnerability creates connection faster than almost

anything. I don't remember where I read it, but I love the definition that says "intimacy = into-me-see."

One morning, my younger daughter, Clancy, came downstairs and sat on the couch beside me. I could tell she was upset even before she said, "Mama, you taught me that if we bring sin into the light, that it takes away its power. I can't keep this inside me anymore. I need to get it out." Clancy proceeded to confess her struggle and failure in an area.

Although she was sixteen years old at the time, I scooped her up, put her in my lap, and held on tightly. I kissed the top of her head and thanked her for trusting me enough to invite me into her hidden places. I assured her that her imperfection only made me love her more.

She looked at me with tears in her eyes and said, "I think some mothers think they give birth to angels, and then when they mess up they think they are more like fallen angels. I'm glad that you know you gave birth to a human."

That touched my heart deeply. Isn't that what we all want? To be seen, in all our glory, for better or for worse; for the good, the bad, and the ugly—and to still be embraced and kissed and held?

—Friendship for Grown-Ups

Father, I am so grateful that you see me for who I am . . . and still you draw me in your loving embrace. I can go forward this week with confidence, knowing that no matter how I feel, you are greater than my feelings.

God's GPS

by Lisa Harper

Your own ears will hear him. Right behind you a voice will say, "This is the way you should go," whether to the right or to the left.

ISAIAH 30:21

God gives us specific directions—even when life is loud and chaotic. All we have to do is listen.

I hate to admit it, but the most recent place I heard divine GPS (I've intentionally rechristened that term to mean "God's Positioning System" because the lady who lives in my dashboard has an annoying voice unlike the pleasant tone of the Holy Spirit in my head) was in the drive-thru line at Taco Bell.

I was in a hurry as usual and the joint that blessed the world with the bazillion-calorie-Doritos-inspired taco was the only place I had time to grab a bite before racing into another meeting. So I wheeled into their drive-thru and while I was pondering the menu in front of me, a very sweet voice piped out of the metal talk box:

"Welcome to Taco Bell, may I take your order, please?" I was surprised by the genuine kindness in the disembodied voice so I said, "You sure can! I want one of those little plain bean burritos and a Diet Pepsi, please." Then I pulled around the corner to meet the person the voice lived in.

The first thing I noticed was that she had a wide smile, which in my experience is an atypical expression for a teenager working the drive-thru window. I'm more used to sullen and clipped with a side order of rolled eyes. In that exact moment, I sensed God poking me and whispering, *She could use a little encouragement today, Lisa.* So, I said, "You have a great voice and a wonderful smile. What's your name?" To which she grinned wider and said, "My name is Leondria." I asked, "Lee-Own-Dree-Ah?" She replied firmly, "No, Lee-Awn-Dree-Uh." Then I said, "Lee-Awn-Dree-Uh, you remind me of a verse in the Bible that says, 'Those who look to him are radiant; their faces are never covered with shame' (Psalm 34:5, NIV)."

Of course, we'd only known each other for thirty seconds, so I wasn't sure how well the affirmation would go over. But then in a tumble of words Leondria told me it was her eighteenth birthday and she'd been bummed all afternoon because she really wanted to be hanging out with her friends instead of being stuck in a Taco Bell drive-thru.

She explained that she'd just been thinking, *Lawd, I need some kind of reminder that you see me today, because this ain't exactly how I wanted to spend my birthday*, before I appeared. Her eyes lit up as she exclaimed, "Then he sent me *you* to remind me of how special I am!" And for a minute there I thought she was going to try and squeeze through that itty-bitty window to hug me.

—Overextended . . . and Loving Most of It!

Father, thank you that you see when I need encouragement— and that you care enough to send it my way. Help me to listen when you whisper in my ear so that I can encourage others I meet as I go through my day.

The Woman No One Knew

by Kristina Gantt

Two people are better off than one, for they can help each other succeed. If one person falls, the other can reach out and help.

ECCLESIASTES 4:9-10

Several years ago, I went to my very first Women of Faith event. I had just left my job of fifteen years to be a stay-at-home mom and full-time photographer. We have lived in the same small town for many years; however, I had always worked, so I did not really know too many women my age except through my job. Making the change from working and having coworkers as my friends to knowing *no* one on a friend level was very hard.

I was a closed-up person anyway, so not getting too close to people was *no* problem. I could not get close to other women because I had been raped at seventeen, married at eighteen, and abused and divorced with two children by twenty-four. *No one* knew my life—and I liked it that way.

But we all know that you have to have other women with whom you can talk so you can make it through hard times. When you can share your stories, you know you are not the only one in the world going through challenges in life. You have to allow God to start breaking down those brick walls, and that is what he started doing with me.

Sunday church rolled around, and a woman in my Sunday school class told me about the Women of Faith event in Atlanta and asked if I wanted to go. The first thing I found myself saying was, "How does this work?" She said, "Carpool and just enjoy a girls' weekend full of Christian women." After about a week, I decided to go. However, I would drive myself—this way I did not have to get close to any woman, and there would be no discussions or questions about my personal life.

The first night was amazing. I could feel the Lord speaking to my heart on so many levels. By the second day I was in tears. I called my husband—who knows just how much of a closed-up person I am—and said, "I am so sorry for putting you through my hard times and not always being the wife you need." I could feel the care in his voice when he said, "That is what I am here for. . . . And I love you no matter what walls you put up."

The Lord put that one person in Sunday school in my path for a special reason. Years later, I am a very different woman of God. I talk to other women about things I have been through and how God has never left my side, even when I thought he had. The women who encouraged me to go are some of my best friends now.

Father, you know just what I need. Thank you for loving me enough to push me out of my comfort zone when that's what I need to grow.

He Knew Me

by Christine Caine

You saw me before I was born. Every day of my life was recorded in your book. Every moment was laid out before a single day had passed.

PSALM 139:16

Two weeks before my thirty-third birthday, I got a phone call from my older brother, George. "Chris, I got a letter from the government, and it says I've been adopted."

I laughed. Growing up you never think you're related to your siblings. "George, obviously they made a mistake. Call and tell them that they sent this letter to the wrong person."

Ten minutes later he called me back, sobbing. "Chris, it's true. They told me the name of my biological mother, my biological father, when I was born, when I was immunized. I have an entire file of my life. I'm going to go and confront Mom!" We Greeks are extremely volatile; we act first and think later. I jumped in my car and walked into my mother's house right at the moment my brother was giving her the piece of paper.

My mom started sobbing; she said, "George, I am so sorry. We never thought you would find out. One of the last things I promised your daddy before he died was that I would never tell you. So I tore up all of the paperwork and never, ever thought you would find out." It was a very big, fat, Greek moment. My mom was crying, my brother was crying, the dog was crying, snot was flying . . . and being a good Greek daughter, I thought, *I'm going to the kitchen to make baklava; that'll solve everything.*

Fifteen minutes later, my mother came into the kitchen and said, "Christine, since we are telling the truth, do you want to know the whole truth?" I stood there, stunned. "I've been adopted too?" It was a surreal moment.

The first thing that came out of my mouth was "Am I still Greek?" And then the very next thing, right there in my Greek Orthodox mother's kitchen, came the thought: "Before I was formed in my mother's womb—*whose ever womb that was*—he knew me. He knew my innermost thoughts; *he* knitted me together; he fashioned all of my days. I am fearfully and wonderfully made."

That day, every fact that I had thought to be true about my life, my past, and my name changed—but the truth about me did not change. Although I do not know all the facts, there is a force that is much higher than the facts, and that is the truth of the Word of God. And God's Word says that "we are His workmanship, created in Christ Jesus for good works" (Ephesians 2:10, NKJV). The good news is that this same God not only loves me and has a great plan and purpose for *my* life—he has that for every single person on the planet, including you.

—————————————— ✝ ——————————————

Lord, there are unanswered questions I have about my life, my past, and my future. I leave my uncertainties at your feet, and I trust you with the details of my life. I believe you cause everything to work together for my good and for your ultimate purposes to be fulfilled.

I'm Alive and He Loves Me!

by Keisha Krezman

Your Father knows exactly what you need even before you ask him!

MATTHEW 6:8

My mother and I were going on a mother/daughter getaway, and it happened to be to Women of Faith. We were both extremely excited to have the great opportunity to attend and had been looking forward to it for months. We had heard nothing but wonderful things about the experience.

Then four days prior to attending the event, a bombshell hit. I was sat down by my doctor, who told me that the surgery I had undergone two weeks prior, to remove my left ovary full of cysts, had actually removed ovarian tumors. That's right—*tumors*. There were so many unknowns, concerns, and questions, but we packed our bags and headed to Women of Faith.

When we first got there, there was a cloud above us; we could feel it. We got checked into the hotel and went back on the bus to head to the celebration . . . *celebration?* We were not thinking that at the time.

We found our seats, sat down, and just held hands. Then the ballerinas came on stage . . . wow. The beauty they portrayed through their movements was simply astonishing. Both my mom and I broke; we started to cry, fighting every second of it. All I could think was, *This is going to be a long weekend.*

The next day they had all the speakers come out for a Q&A session. One question that came up surprised us: "I was just diagnosed with cancer, and I am wondering how to deal with this."

My mom looked at me. . . . I was like, "*No,* I didn't submit that!"

The answers the speakers and artists gave were astounding. They didn't sugarcoat the fact that it is a process and that there are going to be good and bad days; but they did make it clear that God is *always* there with you. He is walking beside you through it all. Although our circumstances may be tough, they can also be a blessing. The cloud I felt when I first arrived had finally lifted! I can do this! I have a husband who loves me; I have a family who is there for me; but most of all, I *am* walking with God!

Since then many things have happened—still a lot of unknowns—but I have been able to use my experience to share God's love and help others who do not know God see through me that with him all things are possible!

EDITOR'S NOTE: *Since her experience at Women of Faith, Keisha has beaten cancer and—despite being told by doctors that she could not have children—given birth to a healthy set of twins.*

Great are you, Lord, and worthy of my praise. You have promised to never leave me or forsake me. I confess I cannot fathom the mysteries of your will or understand why painful and difficult things come into our lives, but I know this—you are God and you've got this!

Free to Carry Out His Work

by Thelma Wells

Instead, we will speak the truth in love, growing in every way more and more like Christ.

EPHESIANS 4:15

Many people are looking for absolute freedom. Freedom from fear, anxiety, sickness, hopelessness, poverty, ignorance, negative emotions, insecurity, disharmony, joblessness—you name it, we want freedom from it. But we cannot experience complete and total freedom without some constraints. To be free to do whatever we want is to become a slave to laziness and sin.

Our purpose in life is not to shun our responsibilities as model citizens or to become lazy about any other obligations, but to be free to live out our God-given assignments. Jesus knew his purpose well: He came to set the prisoners free.

Hundreds of years before Christ walked this earth, Isaiah prophesied clearly what the Messiah's purpose would be:

> *The Spirit of the Lord GOD is upon Me,*
> *Because the LORD has anointed Me*
> *To preach good tidings to the poor;*
> *He has sent Me to heal the brokenhearted,*
> *To proclaim liberty to the captives,*
> *And the opening of the prison to those who are bound;*
> *To proclaim the acceptable year of the LORD,*
> *And the day of vengeance of our God;*
> *To comfort all who mourn,*
> *To console those who mourn in Zion,*
> *To give them beauty for ashes,*
> *The oil of joy for mourning,*
> *The garment of praise for the spirit of heaviness;*
> *That they may be called trees of righteousness,*
> *The planting of the LORD, that He may be glorified.*
>
> ISAIAH 61:1-3, NKJV

Christ's purpose was the kingdom's work—that is, the work of helping people on this earth. Since we are supposed to emulate Christ, we can join him in the same purpose: to encourage the poor, to speak healing to the brokenhearted, to show the freedom of Jesus to those who do not believe, to enlighten those who are in darkness, to let them know that Jesus lives in our hearts, to be a comfort to those who are hurting and grieving, to spread joy wherever we go, and to praise God in all situations so that people will see the Savior living in us. Christ sent us to be ambassadors for him on earth to help bring others into his kingdom.

God wants us to serve his purpose on the earth and to live with him forever when we die. That's the freedom he gave us on the morning he arose from the grave.

—Amazing Freedom

Dear Jesus, I want to accomplish my purpose on this earth and fulfill my lifework. Open opportunities today for me to minister to others and be of service to you. May my life reflect the love of Christ and love for others. Help me not to be so caught up in my own life and schedule that I fail to see the needs of others.

Free from Fear

by Barbara Johnson

*I am convinced that nothing can ever separate us from
God's love. Neither death nor life, neither angels nor
demons, neither our fears for today nor our worries about
tomorrow—not even the powers of hell can separate us
from God's love.*

ROMANS 8:38

What's keeping you awake at night? What's
stealing your joy and keeping you bound
by fear? Maybe you need to set your mind free from
those chains that bind you to worry and torment. The
prophet Isaiah praised God for keeping "in perfect
peace all who trust in you, whose thoughts are fixed
on you" (26:3). I want to be one of those who snore
through the night in "perfect peace"!

Just think what we can accomplish when we're
freed from fear and worry. One of my friends said she
gained a new understanding of how we live out this

kind of fear-free Christian life when she overheard her kids explaining a video game. "You don't have to worry about risking your life to face the dragon or jump the chasm," her kids said, "because if you play the game right, you've got another life to step into and continue the battle."

When the doctor told me that tests revealed a brain tumor that was probably malignant, he predicted, "These next twenty-four hours, as you adjust to this news, will be the hardest twenty-four hours you've ever lived."

I looked at him and smiled. *Doctor*, I thought, *you obviously know* nothing *about my life!*

At that point, God had already helped me endure enough frightening episodes to prove to me his love and support are steadfast. I'd endured having my husband, Bill, injured so severely in a car crash that doctors predicted he'd be in a vegetative state the rest of his life, then the death of two sons, the estrangement of another son after we argued about his homosexuality, and finally, my own diagnosis of diabetes. And after all that, the doctor thought I'd lose sleep over a brain tumor? Not likely!

God had held my hand as I'd walked through lots of fires before that one. I knew this new furnace experience probably wouldn't be easy, and it certainly wouldn't be pleasant. But I also knew that no matter what happened, I had another life waiting for me to step into. I knew the one who had created me would be with me every step of the way.

And that night, I closed my eyes and enjoyed a good night's sleep, free from fear.

—Amazing Freedom

Dear Lord Jesus, fix my eyes upon you, that I may rest and live in perfect peace. I will never have a problem-free life, but I can have a fear-free life as I depend on you. Only you can turn problems into potential, obstacles into opportunities, and tragedies into triumphs. You are a mighty God, and your love has no limits.

A Clean Slate

by Mary Graham

*If we confess our sins to him, he is faithful and just
to forgive us our sins and to cleanse us from all wickedness.*

1 JOHN 1:9

Every weekend before a Women of Faith event begins, the speakers, guests, and musicians gather in a room backstage to pray. Inevitably, those meetings are punctuated by spontaneous music as someone starts singing a chorus or a verse from an old hymn and everyone else joins in to sing along. We love those gatherings.

Some years ago we were in Denver for an event. As usual, we gathered to pray on Friday night. Joining us that weekend was Ashaley, a young woman from National House of Hope—a residential program for hurting, troubled teens—who was there to tell her story from the platform. Ashaley prayed, "Father, we're all here because you've wiped our slates clean."

I loved that. I noted that this young girl was sharing the platform with the Women of Faith speaker team, Jennifer Rothschild, Nichole Nordeman, and the musicians of Avalon. Everyone else in that lineup has extensive ministry experience and expertise, but Ashaley, a teenage girl, was absolutely accurate. We were all there because of the same reality: God had wiped our slates clean. As diverse as we were individually, we held one thing in common: We'd been forgiven of our sins.

In that moment, as she prayed, Ashaley was leading us all, reminding us of this great truth: "He is so rich in kindness and grace that he purchased our freedom with the blood of his Son and forgave our sins" (Ephesians 1:7). That was the only reason any of us were standing in that room, at that moment, getting ready to go into a crowd of women to talk about what God had done in our lives.

*Heavenly Father, we bring our failures to you in Jesus'
name. We've tried so hard and so often to change, but to
no avail. We throw ourselves totally at your mercy and
thank you for your forgiveness and for "wiping our slates
clean." We choose to walk every day in the Spirit and not
in our flesh so we can know your power at work within
us and live in victory. We rest in your mercy, faithfulness,
and love.*

Love Is a Someone

by Jenna Lucado Bishop

God is love, and all who live in love live in God, and God lives in them.

1 JOHN 4:16

L ove. We were made for it. Made to love. Made to be loved. Made to say love. Made to know . . . Love.

But did you know you were made by love?

Love thought you into existence. Love knit you together in your mother's womb and then breathed life into your soul. Love gave you a purpose. Love gave you a name. Love knows the number of hairs on your head and number of thoughts inside it.

Love knows your every move, your every secret, your every victory, your every tear, your every chuckle, your every sigh. Love made you. You see . . .

Love is a Someone.

Sure, *love* is a word.

You've read the word hundreds of times on hundreds of book covers, billboards, magazines. You've heard the word thousands of times in thousands of song lyrics, commercials, movies. You've said the word millions of times about millions of things, places, people.

Sure, love is an action.

Sure, love comes with feelings. You feel butterflies when he walks into the room. You feel comfortable to be yourself when you are with them. You feel compassion when she is hurting.

But, above all, love is a *Someone*.

First John 4:8: "God *is* love" (emphasis mine).

Get to know the Love that made you. Get to know the only Love who won't fail you.

Sit with God. Soak up God. Spend time with God. Because the more we get to know Love as a Someone, the more we understand what love really means.

—*Love Is . . .*

Father, thank you for reminding me that you don't "just" love, but that you are *love. And you will be with me always.*

Love Who You Are

by Luci Swindoll

The whole law can be summed up in this one command:
"Love your neighbor as yourself."

Perhaps the poet and playwright e. e. cummings said it best: "To be nobody but yourself in a world which is doing its best, night and day, to make you everybody else—means to fight the hardest battle which any human being can fight; and never stop fighting."

Would everybody who loves yourself please raise your hand? Not many hands going up, are there? To love oneself was sort of frowned on when I was young. At least, it wasn't encouraged in Christian circles where I grew up. If the truth were known, we didn't talk about it much. Because conceit, pride, and arrogance were frowned upon, I suppose I equated them with loving yourself. We were taught to put others first, to give place to those around us, and to take a backseat when others were present.

I've lived a long time since then and have had lots of opportunity to rethink this concept of loving who you are. I view it somewhat differently now. I still know conceit, pride, and arrogance are wrong, and I still believe in a servant spirit—more than ever—but I've learned that loving oneself is actually a biblical command. It's stated in an interesting way, so it's often misunderstood—but it's there.

In the book of Matthew, Jesus says, ". . . Love your neighbor as yourself" (19:19; 22:39). And Paul says in Galatians 5:14 that the law is fulfilled when you "love your neighbor as yourself." Again, Romans 13:9 and James 2:8 reiterate the command to love your neighbor as yourself. In every case, loving your neighbor is predicated on loving yourself first.

When e. e. cummings said it's hard to be ourselves, I think he could have just as strongly said it's almost impossible to love ourselves. So often we don't like who we are. We don't like what we see in the mirror, we're dissatisfied with how we look or what we weigh, or we're disappointed in how we've misbehaved or how we've treated someone else. And the sum total of that prevents us from truly loving ourselves.

At one time or another I've felt unlovable for all the reasons listed above, and I imagine you have too. And on rare occasions, I still do. But I've learned that God loves me, no matter what. As long as I am confident in God's love for me, I eventually come around to the realization I can love me, too.

—Life! Celebrate It

Father, your love for me is perfect. Help me to love my loved ones with your perfect love.

Enough

by Shauna Niequist

*Be happy with those who are happy, and weep with those
who weep.*

ROMANS 12:15

At one point I told Aaron that if I found out I wasn't
pregnant that month, I'd break something glass,
just to feel it shatter in my hands. I was counting the
days all the time, recounting, hoping. And then I found
out I wasn't pregnant. Again, I didn't break anything,
but I posted something on my blog about how I was
feeling. I should have been doing all sorts of other,
more urgent work, but that morning at the coffee shop,
all that sadness and frustration and confusion bled out
of my fingers and onto the screen.

Later that week I had lunch with my friend Emily.
She lives in Michigan and came in town to visit. To be
honest, I hoped she hadn't read my post. She was one

of my seventeen pregnant friends, and I wanted to talk about her baby and pregnancy—about cravings and names and maternity clothes. I wanted it to be a sweet, happy lunch. And it was. We talked about all the lovely baby stuff, and then she gave me a card and a gift.

She told me that she had read my post and that this was the point in friendship when sometimes two friends walk away from each other for a while, because the pain and the awkwardness and the tenderness was too great. She said she thought we could do better than that.

And then she handed me two pairs of safety goggles.

She said, "When you feel like shattering something, I'll be right there with you. We'll put on our safety goggles. I'll help you break something, and then I'll help you clean it up."

She said, "You've been celebrating with me, and I'll be here to grieve with you. We can do this together."

It took my breath away. We cried together at the restaurant, the two of us, one pregnant, one not, sitting next to the window of an Italian restaurant on a busy street, each with a pair of Home Depot safety goggles, tears running down our faces.

It was one of the most extraordinary experiences of friendship I've ever had. Because it would have been so easy for her to say "I'm in my happy season. This is a wonderful, blessed season for me, and I don't want Angry Pants over here wrecking it." She could have concluded it was so complicated to manage her joy and my sadness that she wouldn't enter into this mess. But she did enter in.

Something broke inside me that day. Something cracked, and all the energy and fear and roiling anger drained out. I felt calm and empty. I felt sad but not devastated. I was exhausted and could not carry it anymore.

Enough.

—*Bread & Wine*

Father, the love of a friend is such a gift. Thank you for the friends you've placed in my life. Help me to love them well.

$\left(\text{WINTER} \right)$

This Is What Love Looks Like

by Patsy Clairmont

No one has ever seen God. But if we love each other, God lives in us, and his love is brought to full expression in us.

1 JOHN 4:12

Love can be smoochy, like a nana's kisses, or it can be stout, like a grandfather's handshake. Love can be life-giving, like a parent's approval, or nurturing, like a teacher's praise. Love can be tender, like a sweetheart's embrace, or tough, like a coach's instructions. However it is packaged, one thing we know . . . love matters.

Through the nineteen years ladies have been attending Women of Faith, the one word we—the speaking team, concourse team, and office team—have heard repeatedly is how loved you have felt while attending. We are so grateful, because from the beginning, whether we were talking or singing about joy or heartbreak, our foundation has been the love of God in Christ Jesus our Lord. Because we know it is his love that changes our lives.

We cannot begin to express our gratefulness for your participation and ongoing support through attendance, volunteering, and letters. I can still remember watching from behind the curtains as thousands of you spilled down into the arenas. My heart thumped with excitement and stage jitters to think of how privileged I was to be a part of this. The speaker team would circle in prayer, asking God to make himself known personally, intimately, and eternally in every life.

One Women of Faith participant who eventually became a friend attended for years on a gurney with portable life support and a team of nurses so she might hear words of hope. She had ALS but was determined to live out her years with faith. We were inspired by her courage. Many of you came to us while in the midst of great trials and losses. It would break our hearts to hear you whisper in our ears at break time of how you had just buried your child, or lost your home, or received a staggering health diagnosis. We knew we didn't have the power to change your story, but we also knew the Author and Finisher of our lives could and would walk with you, and comfort you, and love on you. Our responsibility was to be his arms, his voice, and his spirit of encouragement for the hours we shared.

It was amazing how cold arenas became warm sanctuaries as your praise rose to fill the buildings with acknowledgement (of God's authority), gratitude (for his provision), and longing (to know him more deeply). Our many speakers and dramatists spoke from their experiences and connected with you. We know that because you told us in evaluations, phone calls, and letters how in the midst of thousands you felt the speaker talking directly to you. That was the personalization of God's Spirit. That was Love.

And now we celebrate that God allowed us this incredible journey of years spent lifting up the loving name of his dear Son and our Savior, Jesus. Thank you for being our friends.

Always remember: You are loved.

Father, thank you for loving me. It makes all the difference. As I go through this week, help me to remember that no matter what may happen, I can always count on your love for me.

She Could Not Go Unnoticed

by Sandi Patty

*Jesus said, "Someone deliberately touched me, for I felt
healing power go out from me." When the woman realized
that she could not stay hidden, she began to tremble and fell
to her knees in front of him. The whole crowd heard her
explain why she had touched him and that she had been
immediately healed. "Daughter," he said to her, "your faith
has made you well. Go in peace."*

LUKE 8:46-48

There's [a] story in the Bible about a woman falling forward, in the right direction, toward Jesus.
She had some kind of a disease that involved bleeding,
and for twelve years she had consulted every healer
imaginable. No one had been able to help her, and I can
just imagine how desperate she must have been! When
she heard Jesus was coming to town, she must have
known He was her last hope. But He was surrounded

by crowds, and in the crush of people, she could not get His attention. She barely managed to simply touch the edge of His garment—and she was healed! Not only that, Jesus stopped in His tracks, having felt some power go out of Him, and asked that whoever had touched Him would *reveal* themselves.

Luke 8:47 says, "Then the woman, seeing that she could not go unnoticed, came trembling and fell at his feet. In the presence of all the people, she told why she had touched him and how she had been instantly healed" (NIV). I love that phrase, "the woman saw that *she could not go unnoticed.*" Jesus sees and notices every little thing about us. Jesus saw her and felt compassion for her, and the power went out of Him to cure her. The woman was rewarded by her choice to *reveal herself,* and Jesus told her, "Your faith has healed you" (Luke 8:48).

All that stuff we think we are hiding is actually an open book before His compassionate eyes anyway. So you might as well just relax, open up, and let the Healer do His job and start the process of setting you free. Allow the Great Physician to do any surgery He needs to do to remove old infested wounds that are holding you back.

—Falling Forward

Heavenly Father, thank you that I don't need to jump through hoops to get your attention. Help me reach out to you when I have wounds that need your healing touch.

God with Skin On

by Sheila Walsh

"I will comfort those who mourn, bringing words of praise to their lips. May they have abundant peace, both near and far," says the LORD, who heals them.

ISAIAH 57:18-19

I had decided to take an hour away from my to-do list and have a pedicure. I melted into the seat, plopped my feet into a bath of fragrant warm water, and closed my eyes. I resisted the nail technician's insistence that everyone should choose red polish at Christmas.

"Miss Sheila, you must wear red; it's the holidays!"

"That's not in the Bible," I replied, giving her my purple polish.

"Ah, you crazy!" she replied, not for the first time.

I began to drift away when I heard someone say, "You look just like Sheila Walsh." I opened my eyes and turned to the woman who was now sitting in the chair beside me.

"Oh, you are Sheila Walsh!" she said. We chatted for a few moments, and she told me that she had attended a couple of our conferences and how much they had helped her. We talked about our children, and she told me that she has three young ones.

"They must be excited," I said.

"Christmas will be different for us this year," she replied. "My husband died of brain cancer."

"I'm so sorry," I said. "When did he die?"

"Yesterday."

We sat in silence for a few moments. I was stunned at the immediacy of this loss. My heart ached for her and for her children.

"Our church has been wonderful in every way," she said. "I have seen God's love in action."

I told her of God's amazing faithfulness to my mom when she was left with three children to raise after my father's death. God's presence was so evident as we sat together, two women with their feet in tubs of hot water, their hearts in the hands of the King of kings, holding hands across a tray of nail polish.

I was finished first and went to wash my hands.

When I got back she was gone, but there was a note for me. She wrote that even as she drove to the salon that morning she had prayed for peace and protection and thanked God that he sat us next to each other. "I just needed a touch of God with skin on."

That day was a reminder that God never takes his eyes off us; he sees us and cares about us. He saw this exhausted, heartbroken woman as she drove to a nail salon, a brief respite before the evening's wake for her beloved husband, and he sat her beside a sister in God's family with skin on.

—Contagious Joy

Father, I know you see me in my hour of need, whenever and wherever that might be. Thank you for the times you send someone "with skin on" to remind me you are always there for me.

Witness to His Love

by Lisa Lynn

*I will be glad and rejoice in your unfailing love, for you
have seen my troubles, and you care about the anguish
of my soul.*

PSALM 31:7

I left the Women of Faith event a few years ago having actually acknowledged my own hurt, shame,
etc., from being molested repeatedly as a child. I no
longer just held a secret . . . I started to heal.

In earlier years, I would periodically pray for my
abuser—I prayed that person would die. Now it was
different. Something inside told me that while my
abuser was wrong, I didn't know the life they may have
experienced. I did not want to be their judge. Instead
I asked God to help the abuser recognize their wrongs
and accept the Lord's grace and forgiveness. Within
sixty days of that prayer, I found out that my abuser
suddenly *had* died. I got up the courage to go to the

visitation and look into the casket so I could say, "I forgave you."

I was almost hyperventilating as the minister gently assisted me, the last in the line, into the church. I didn't know how to say, "I'm not here to go to the funeral," so I sat at the very back awaiting my escape. The service was different from any I had been to before; it began by the minister talking about how "the church would never know what brought this hurting soul here about sixty days ago."

What? Sixty days ago?

The minister then spoke of the change this individual went through. He spoke of the sorrows and the pain this person had caused to others . . . and the tears this person had shed. Next he spoke of the joy my abuser found in the Lord (and in dancing). The minister indicated that many people had been brought to the Lord through this very sinner and asked them to stand up. I could not believe my eyes. There were about a dozen people who stood and gave their testimonies of change. They spoke about how they had come to the

Lord and had found comfort in the forgiveness of Jesus and his love—things they learned of from my abuser.

God allowed me to witness this, even when I had wanted to run. I saw evidence of his love, his ability to change someone, his right to judge, the joy found in dancing, and the healing found in forgiveness.

It reminded me of that day at Women of Faith. As I released the secret that was crushing my soul, I received the truth in return: Nobody can change us except God.

Heavenly Father, I want to be open to the changes you want to make in my heart. Help me forgive those who have wronged me and to see them as you do—as deeply loved.

Letters to Read on a Bad Day

by Leslie Nunn Reed

Let's not get tired of doing what is good. At just the right time we will reap a harvest of blessing if we don't give up.

GALATIANS 6:9

My first job out of college gave me the opportunity to work for a gifted entrepreneur who taught me so many things about running a business, developing client relationships, and leading people.

One day, while flipping through a file drawer, I spotted a folder labeled "Letters to Read on a Bad Day." My boss said she had created it after deciding to save a nice letter she received on a day that wasn't going so well. Twenty-five years later, she still has the file and peeks inside when she needs a lift.

I don't recall when I started a folder like that of my own, but over the years I've tucked in notes, letters, e-mails, and cards sent from friends, colleagues, and clients. During seasons of discouragement or disappointment, I've pulled open the drawer and cracked open the folder.

What greets me is a shower of encouragement, appreciation, and thankfulness—for work I've done or perhaps the way I've done it. For making the investment to get to know a new friend or for allowing myself to *be* known in a relationship—even in the midst of my uncertainties and insecurities.

Though the kind wishes written in the notes are intended for me, I find myself responding with immense gratitude to God that I invested in these relationships, organizations, and causes. That my gifts and talents made some kind of positive difference. That my contribution was worthwhile.

In the rereading, my "bad day" quickly brightens. My perspective shifts. My outlook changes. My focus turns from thinking about what went wrong to seeing what might be possible. Bits of paper and ink carry treasured reminders that what we do matters.

You may not think you have a similar file of encouraging correspondence, but you do: The Bible is filled with "letters" to God's children. He knew the challenges the people within its pages faced and dealt with them tenderly. He also knows the challenges we face today. The amazing thing about Scripture is that the words that encouraged and inspired readers thousands of years ago can speak into our lives in ways that would probably have astonished the original writers.

What a gift from such a giver. It's a great reminder to pull out those Words—on "good" days and "bad"— to discover the truths and messages just for you.

Dear God, thank you for tucking encouraging messages in your Word for me to find. Help me remember to look for them when my day is filled with challenges. Remind me to send my words of appreciation and encouragement to others so that I might help brighten their not-so-great days.

The Hairs on Our Heads

by Susan Ellingburg

What is the price of two sparrows—one copper coin? But not a single sparrow can fall to the ground without your Father knowing it. And the very hairs on your head are all numbered. So don't be afraid; you are more valuable to God than a whole flock of sparrows.

MATTHEW 10:29-31

One morning during my usual getting-ready-for-work routine, I paused long enough to pull an enormous handful of hair out of my hairbrush. That's not normally something I spend a lot of time pondering, but that morning I had three distinct thoughts:

One: Should I be worried about this?

Two: With all this hair apparently falling out of my head, how is it that I am not bald already?

Three: Doesn't the Bible say something about God knowing the number of hairs on our heads?

It turns out that in both the books of Matthew and Luke, Jesus shares that the hairs on our heads are numbered. (I wonder if they fall out in numerical order?) I used to think of this as just one more entry in my official file, noted on a vital stats form under "Hairs (number)," and neatly tucked away in a heavenly file cabinet. But judging from my hairbrush, the number of hairs on my head varies from day to day, even moment to moment.

So how can God know how many there are at any given time? Only by paying constant attention to this small, intimate detail of our lives. How amazing is it that while God is dealing with national, international, and even galactic issues, he still manages to keep track of each little hair on your head? He even knows their original color.

What's more remarkable, to my mind, is not just that God *can* know how many hairs our heads are sporting at any given moment, but that he actually notes the number. If God cares enough to keep track of your follicle count, do you think that he would ignore larger issues like health scares, financial crises, relationship dramas, or whatever it is that has you ready to tear your hair out?

The next time you brush a loose strand off your shoulder, remember that your heavenly Father knew the exact moment that hair "let go." Then take a moment to thank the one who knows you best for his watchful, unfailing love.

Father, your attention to detail blows me away. I don't understand how you can care so much about even the tiniest detail of my life, but I am humbled and grateful that you do.

Ready to Fight

by Jenny Neighbour

Your Father already knows your needs. Seek the Kingdom of God above all else, and he will give you everything you need.

LUKE 12:30-31

I had always believed in God, but I didn't "know him" very well. Early in my marriage I found myself in a "mommy's Bible study" group filled with other young mothers trying to find their way through a life filled with kids, husbands, jobs, and learning about this God thing. I felt truly blessed to have this amazing group of women in my life.

Then, something horrible happened. A woman in our group was diagnosed with stage four breast cancer. She was barely thirty years old and had four little girls to raise. We didn't know how to help. What do you do for a dear friend with a horrible diagnosis and very little hope for survival?

I was half paying attention to the TV when I

heard an ad for a Women of Faith event in St. Paul, Minnesota. It stopped me dead in my tracks: uplifting music, Christian comedy, dramas, real-life stories, fun with girlfriends. Are you kidding me? That sounded amazing! I just knew that we *had* to get Bonnie to this event.

It was easy to convince the girls to join me; Bonnie was especially eager to get out of town and do something to help take her mind off things. So we hopped in the church van and headed on a four-hour trip to St. Paul. Keep in mind that I had never been to a Women of Faith event in my life, and all of my friends were counting on *me* to make this weekend amazing for Bonnie. No pressure, right? I was so nervous. Would this help Bonnie find some peace? Would it be "too much" for us "new believers"?

We came into the arena scared, but less than ten minutes into the event, we started to feel comfortable. Then it was time for a drama. Are you ready for this? They made the stage look like a boxing ring, and Nicole Johnson came out in boxing attire . . . gloves and all. And what she was fighting? *Breast cancer*!

Really, God? How did you know?

On the way home it was very quiet in the van. I was scared to ask Bonnie how she felt. Did we do the right thing by bringing her? When I finally asked, she said without hesitation, "I know this event will not *heal* me . . . but I know this . . . I am ready to *fight* this battle now! I know that no matter what, God will be with me." We didn't know how to help Bonnie, but God knew exactly what she needed.

Dear God, I know that you are for me! You have gone to extraordinary lengths to pursue me and have a relationship with me. I want to grow in my relationship with you and with others. Help me to develop godly friendships and seek out others who may need you in their lives.

Cold Tangerines

by Shauna Niequist

Oh, that you would choose life, so that you and your descendants might live!

DEUTERONOMY 30:19

I've missed whole seasons of my life. I look back and all I remember is pain. I guess I went to work or to class during that time, but I don't really remember. I wasted a lot of time wishing I was different. I didn't love the gift of life because I was too busy being angry about the life I was given. I wanted it to be different. But being angry didn't change those things. It just wasted time. I can't take away the things that have happened to you or to me, but what we have, maybe as a reward for getting through all the other days, is today. Today is a gift. And if we have tomorrow, tomorrow will be a gift.

It's rebellious, in a way, to choose joy, to choose to dance, to choose to love your life. It's much easier and much more common to be miserable. But I choose to do what I can do to create hope, to celebrate life, and the act of celebrating connects me back to that life I love. We could just live our normal, day-to-day lives, saving all the good living up for someday, but I think today, just plain today, is worth it. I think it's our job, each of us, to live each day like it's a special occasion, because we've been given a gift. We get to live in this beautiful world. When I live purposefully and well, when I dance instead of sitting out, when I let myself laugh hard, when I wear my favorite shoes on a regular Tuesday, that regular Tuesday is better.

Right now, around our house, all the leaves are falling, and there's no reason that they have to turn electric bright red before they fall, but they do, and I want to live like that. I want to say, "What can I do today that brings more beauty, more energy, more hope?" Because it seems like that's what God is saying to us, over and over. "What can I do today to remind you again how good this life is? You think the color of the sky is good now, wait till sunset. You think oranges are good? Try a tangerine." He's a crazy delightful mad scientist and keeps coming back from the lab with great, unbelievable new things, and it's a gift. It's a gift to be a part of it.

I want a life that sizzles and pops and makes me laugh out loud. And I don't want to get to the end, or to tomorrow even, and realize that my life is a collection of meetings and pop cans and errands and receipts and dirty dishes. I want to eat cold tangerines and sing loud in the car with the windows open and wear pink shoes and stay up all night laughing and paint my walls the exact color of the sky right now. I want to sleep hard on clean white sheets and throw parties and eat ripe tomatoes and read books so good they make me jump up and down and I want my everyday to make God belly laugh, glad that He gave life to someone who loves the gift, who will use it up and wring it out and drag it around like a favorite sweater.

Cold Tangerines

Dear Jesus, your Word reminds us that you have come that we may have life, and have it abundantly. I don't want to miss one thing you have for me, or to waste one more minute feeling sorry for myself because things didn't turn out the way I planned. I want to live life to the fullest . . . starting today!

Freedom to Go On

by Luci Swindoll

Dear brothers and sisters, when troubles of any kind come your way, consider it an opportunity for great joy. For you know that when your faith is tested, your endurance has a chance to grow. So let it grow, for when your endurance is fully developed, you will be perfect and complete, needing nothing. If you need wisdom, ask our generous God, and he will give it to you. He will not rebuke you for asking.

JAMES 1:2-5

Nothing in our lives is wasted. Not one thing that happens is without worth somewhere down the road. But we often miss it because we "travel the beaten path" and fail to open our eyes to the outlandish ways God wants to speak to us and love us and change us. We don't recognize the value in celebrating the strange twists, the difficulties, the so-called failures, when we really should . . . and could. We consider our flops or hard times a defeat, but in reality they are God's greatest compliments. They're transforming love gifts from a gracious heavenly Father.

There's an account of this very point in *Say Please, Say Thank You* by Donald McCullough. The Ore-Ida frozen potato company celebrates anniversaries of failures. (They're the folks who make French fries, etc., and they're famous for innovative, creative ideas.) But what do they do when one of those ideas bombs? Do they blame or fire somebody? No, they throw a party! Literally. A cannon is fired and everybody stops work to commemorate the "perfect failure." Together they rejoice in what they've learned. They talk about what will not work, reveling in the fact that no more time, energy, or money has to be spent on a thankless project. They "celebrate their freedom to go on."

I'm not advocating a Pollyanna approach to life. That's totally unrealistic. We all go through terrible times of anxiety and loss—very real pain that takes time to go away, if it ever does. But there's a big difference between that and crawling under the house when things don't go our way or when our path takes what appears to be a too-outlandish turn.

If you wake up tomorrow with a thought that seems just a little bit crazy, or if a loved one brings your ego down to earth with a thud, take heart. It's God's complimentary gift to remind you who's in charge, who gives you freedom to go on . . . and who loves you with an outlandish love.

—*Boundless Love*

Heavenly Father, you are my refuge and my strength and a very present help in times of trouble. I pray you would direct my path today and help me walk in truth. Give me an undivided heart, that I may honor you in all I do. Thank you that failure is never final with you, because you use all things for our benefit.

We Are Not the Problem

by Jen Hatmaker

I saw heaven opened, and a white horse was standing there.
Its rider was named Faithful and True, for he judges fairly
and wages a righteous war. His eyes were like flames of fire,
and on his head were many crowns. A name was written on
him that no one understood except himself. He wore a robe
dipped in blood, and his title was the Word of God.

REVELATION 19:11-13

Hear this: I don't think God wants you at war with yourself.

He sent the Prince of Peace to soothe those tumultuous waters already. Self-depreciation is a cruel response to Jesus, who died and made us righteous. Guilt is not Jesus' medium. He is battling for global redemption right now; His objective hardly includes huddling in the corner with us, rehashing our shame again. He finished that discussion on the cross. Plus, there's no time for that.

We're so conditioned to being a problem that we've forgotten we're actually the answer. God is not angry at you; how could He possibly be? You are His daughter, His son; you're on the team. Don't imagine He is sitting us all down for a lecture. Rather, He's staging a rally, gathering the troops. The church is rising like a phoenix right now, collecting speed and strength and power.

Jesus is staging a massive movement to bind up the brokenhearted and proclaim freedom for captives. The trumpet is blowing. We are on the cusp, on the side of the Hero. So while we're mistakenly warring with ourselves, Jesus is waging war on injustice and calling us to join Him.

This is way more fun than self-condemnation, no?

So imagine me linking arms with you, giving you an affectionate Texas squeeze. Guilt might be the first chapter, but it makes for a terrible story. Jesus gave us lots of superior material to work with. If your stuff and spending and waste and stress are causing you tension like mine is, just do the next right thing. Ask some new questions; conversation partners are everywhere (their name is Legion, for they are many). Take a little baby step. Tomorrow, you can take another. Offer yourself the same grace Jesus has given you. We're no good to Him stuck in paralysis.

—7

Father, I claim my victory, in Jesus' name! Help me to see myself as you see me and to act in ways that are worthy of my calling and honoring to you. Forgive me for listening to myself and "my feelings," and give me ears that hear your voice only, and a heart that quickly obeys.

Dumpster Diving

by Mary Graham

Help him to defend the poor, to rescue the children
of the needy.

PSALM 72:4

Every now and then something happens, and I
know, right then and there, I'll never forget it.
One of those times was at a Women of Faith event in
Spokane, Washington.

That year we placed the folders of World Vision
children in bright orange bags and placed them on
the seats. On Friday night I encouraged the women
to help us change the world for these children who do
not have even the necessities of life available to them.
As the sponsor of a child, you or I can provide clean
water, nutritious food, health care, and education—all

of which will save some of their lives, or at least help ensure their futures.

Having been involved in the work of World Vision for many years, we on the Women of Faith team are very emotional, even passionate, about getting help for these children. So everywhere we go, we talk to everyone who will listen and ask them to join us in helping change the world by providing for children, one life at a time.

I told the women to leave the World Vision bags containing the picture folders in the arena so they wouldn't get lost in the shuffle. Saturday morning, I planned to remind everyone of the bags and invite them to sponsor a child.

But that weekend, contrary to the direction they'd been given, the custodial staff cleaned the arena bowl late Friday night after we'd gone, throwing all the World Vision bags into the garbage. We arrived on Saturday morning to discover a perfectly clean arena— cleared of all the bags and all the children who might have been sponsored that day! To say we were horrified (as well as brokenhearted) would be an understatement.

Without a word, the Women of Faith staff and pro-
duction crew donned masks and gloves and headed for
the trash bins. They painstakingly searched through
the rubbish, looking for bright orange bags. As they
discovered each bag, they sanitized it and readied it for
the World Vision tables.

When the program began, they'd recovered thousands of babies. It was such a metaphor to consider
these dear children being rescued out of the garbage
so they could be claimed by one of the Women of
Faith attendees that day.

I'll never forget how everyone responded: the
heartfelt tears by many at the thought of losing the
opportunity to have the children sponsored; the hard
work of the staff and crew who were willing to find
the bags—even at the bottom of garbage contain-
ers full of food, drink, and who knows what; and the
miracle God gave us as we were reminded that he rescues those who've been abandoned. There are times he
rescues us in more ways than one.

Father, thank you that you never abandon me. You care for me every day in every way.

Breaking the Heart of God

by Marilyn Meberg

I have chosen you and will not throw you away.

ISAIAH 41:9

We are not mass produced. We are one-of-a-kind creations over whom God always has a loving and watchful eye. He calls us by name. He knows how many hairs are on our heads; He knows when we stand up and when we sit down. He is never indifferent to any hurt, challenge, or joy we experience in life. His ear is ever inclined toward our voice when we call out to Him.

And yet, how easily and frequently we can break the heart of God by not responding to His offer of love for each one of us personally designed, one-of-a-kind creations. The most poignant image of breaking

207

the heart of God is provided for us as we read the
words of Jesus looking out over the city of Jerusalem:

> *O Jerusalem, Jerusalem, the city that kills the
> prophets and stones God's messengers! How often
> I have wanted to gather your children together as
> a hen protects her chicks beneath her wings, but
> you wouldn't let me. (Matthew 23:37)*

We have all had our hearts broken by someone who
did not choose us, or by someone who rejected our
offer of love that would have brought the fulfillment
of a relationship. Some of us have even said under
our breath, "It's your loss. I would have been good for
you. We could have had a great life together, but . . .
oh, well."

God never says, "Oh, well." He is relentless in His
love pursuit of us while at the same time honoring
our rights to say, "No, I'm not interested." But just as
Jesus's heart was broken as He said to Jerusalem, "You
wouldn't let me," so it breaks the heart of God when
we don't let Him fulfill His desires for us.

Let me say yet again: meaning for life comes when we realize God made us because He wanted to. First John 4:10 states "not that we loved God, but that he loved us." God made the first move; we choose whether to make the next one.

My prayer for you is that you choose to accept the very reason for which you were born and that you rest in your place of one whom God will never abandon . . . never throw away.

—*Love Me, Never Leave Me*

Father, I never want to cause you pain, and yet I know I sometimes do. Please forgive me. Help me to snuggle next to you, safe under the wings of your love.

You Are Loved

by Sheila Walsh

The Father himself loves you dearly because you love me.

JOHN 16:27

I will never forget a woman I met at the end of a
Women of Faith conference in 1998. She looked to
be about eighty years old. At first she couldn't talk to
me; she simply held my hand and wept. She reminded
me of my grandmother, and I took her in my arms and
held her for a while. When she was able to speak, this
is what she said:

"I've gone to church all my life. But this is the first
time I really understood that God loves me. Not just
everybody . . . but *me*. He really loves *me!*"

I thought about that woman a lot after that night.
How would it have affected her life if she had understood as a child that she was profoundly loved by God?

How would it affect all of our lives if we understood how passionately we are loved by God? I am convinced that we have captured only the smallest glimpse of who Christ really is. I am sure that when we are finally Home, we will be overwhelmed by how little we understood on earth.

Think of John, Christ's beloved disciple. He was perhaps the closest friend of Jesus on this earth. He was probably no more than eighteen years old when he became a disciple. He was the only one at the foot of the cross when Jesus was crucified. He was the second to arrive at the tomb after Christ had risen. He saw it all.

But as Scripture records the rest of John's journey through life, we find him many years later on the Isle of Patmos, a Roman penal colony, the Alcatraz of the Aegean Sea. He is seventy-five or eighty years old. He is near the end of his life, the end of his ministry, the end of the road. But God chose this man, at this moment in his life, to receive what we now know as "The Revelation"—the glorious picture of Christ's Kingdom yet to come.

I used to think that if I had only been there

with Christ, seen the dead raised with my own eyes, experienced the miracles, then my life would be different. Now I don't think so. John knew Christ as well as a human being could, but when he saw the vision of Christ fully revealed in all his risen glory John said, "When I saw him [Jesus], I fell at his feet as though dead. Then he placed his right hand on me and said: 'Do not be afraid. I am the First and the Last. I am the Living One; I was dead, and behold I am alive for ever and ever! And I hold the keys of death and Hades'" (Revelation 1:17-18, NIV).

My friends, we have not even begun to fathom the breadth and the length and the height and the depth of the love and majesty of God. He is the Alpha and Omega, the beginning and the end. Circumstances will not dictate the days of your life, God will. God, in his boundless love, will carry you safely Home into eternity in his glorious presence.

And so we leave you with this immutable truth: You are loved. You are loved. You are loved.

—*Boundless Love*

Father, it's hard to fathom that you really love me. Help me understand . . . and help me share your love with people you bring my way who need to know how much they are loved.

Acknowledgments

Grateful acknowledgment is made to the following authors and publishers for permission to reprint copyrighted material:

Bishop, Jenna Lucado. *Love Is . . . Six Lessons on What Love Looks Like.* Copyright © 2013 by Jenna Lucado Bishop, used under license with Thomas Nelson, a division of HarperCollins Christian Publishing, Inc., www.thomasnelson.com. All rights reserved.

Clairmont, Patsy. "Unstrung." In *Boundless Love: Devotions to Celebrate God's Love for You.* Copyright © 2001 by Women of Faith, Inc., used under license with The Zondervan Corporation, a subsidiary of HarperCollins Christian Publishing, Inc., www.zondervan.com. All rights reserved.

Clairmont, Patsy. "Measuring Up." In *Infinite Grace: The Devotional.* Copyright © 2008 by Patsy Clairmont, Mary Graham, Nicole Johnson, Carol Kent, Marilyn Meberg,

Lucado, Max. *You'll Get Through This: Hope and Help for Your Turbulent Times.* Copyright © 2013 by Max Lucado, used under license with Thomas Nelson, a division of HarperCollins Christian Publishing, Inc., www.thomasnelson.com. All rights reserved.

Mason, Babbie. *This I Know For Sure: Taking God at His Word.* Copyright © 2013 by Abingdon Press.

Meberg, Marilyn. *Love Me, Never Leave Me: Discovering the Inseparable Bond That Our Hearts Crave.* Copyright © 2008 by Marilyn Meberg, used under license with Thomas Nelson, a division of HarperCollins Christian Publishing, Inc., www.thomasnelson.com. All rights reserved.

Meberg, Marilyn. *Tell Me Everything: How You Can Heal from the Secrets You Thought You'd Never Share.* Copyright © 2010 by Marilyn Meberg, used under license with Thomas Nelson, a division of HarperCollins Christian Publishing, Inc., www.thomasnelson.com. All rights reserved.

Miller, Ellen. *The One Year Book of Inspiration for Girlfriends* by Ellen Miller. Copyright © 2009. Used by permission of Tyndale House Publishers, Inc. All rights reserved.

Niequist, Shauna. *Bread & Wine: A Love Letter to Life around the Table, with Recipes.* Copyright © 2013 by Shauna Niequist, used under license with The Zondervan Corporation, a subsidiary of HarperCollins Christian Publishing, Inc., www.zondervan.com. All rights reserved.

Niequist, Shauna. *Cold Tangerines: Celebrating the Extraordinary Nature of Everyday Life.* Copyright © 2007 by Shauna Niequist, used under license with The Zondervan Corporation, a subsidiary of HarperCollins Christian Publishing, Inc., www.zondervan.com. All rights reserved.

Patty, Sandi. *Falling Forward . . . Into His Arms of Grace.* Copyright © 2007 by Sandi Patty, used under license with Thomas Nelson, a division of HarperCollins Christian Publishing, Inc., www.thomasnelson.com. All rights reserved.

Swindoll, Luci. "God's Greatest Compliments." In *Boundless Love: Devotions to Celebrate God's Love for You.* Copyright © 2001 by Women of Faith, Inc., used under license with The Zondervan Corporation, a subsidiary of HarperCollins Christian Publishing, Inc., www.zondervan.com. All rights reserved.

Swindoll, Luci. *Life! Celebrate It: Listen, Learn, Laugh, Love.* Copyright © 2006 by Luci Swindoll, used under license with Thomas Nelson, a division of HarperCollins Christian Publishing, Inc., www.thomasnelson.com. All rights reserved.

Walsh, Sheila. "Conclusion: You Are Loved." In *Boundless Love: Devotions to Celebrate God's Love for You.* Copyright © 2001 by Women of Faith, Inc., used under license with The Zondervan Corporation, a subsidiary of HarperCollins Christian Publishing, Inc., www.zondervan.com. All rights reserved.

Walsh, Sheila. "God's Gift Bearers." In *Contagious Joy: Joyful Devotions to Lift Your Spirits.* Copyright © 2006 by W Publishing Group, used under license with Thomas Nelson, a division of HarperCollins Christian Publishing, Inc., www.thomasnelson.com. All rights reserved.

Walsh, Sheila. *Outrageous Love: A Love That Seeks No Reward.* Copyright © 2004 by Sheila Walsh, used under license with Thomas Nelson, a division of HarperCollins Christian Publishing, Inc., www.thomasnelson.com. All rights reserved.

Wells, Thelma. "Freedom for God's Kingdom Work." In *Amazing Freedom: Devotions to Free Your Spirit and Fill Your Heart.* Copyright © 2006 by Women of Faith, used under license with Thomas Nelson, a division of HarperCollins Christian Publishing, Inc., www.thomasnelson.com. All rights reserved.

Wells, Thelma. *What These Girls Knew: How Girls Back Then Talk to Us Today.* Copyright © 2007 by Thelma Wells, used under license with Thomas Nelson, a division of HarperCollins Christian Publishing, Inc., www.thomasnelson.com. All rights reserved.

Whelchel, Lisa. *Friendship for Grown-Ups: What I Missed and Learned along the Way.* Copyright © 2010 by Lisa Whelchel Cauble, used under license with Thomas Nelson, a division of HarperCollins Christian Publishing, Inc., www.thomasnelson.com. All rights reserved.

Notes

1. Helen Lemmel, "Turn Your Eyes upon Jesus," 1922, public domain.
2. Augustus M. Toplady, "Rock of Ages," 1776, public domain.
3. J. W. Van Deventer, "I Surrender All," 1896, public domain.
4. From a piece in Jenny Holzer's *Living Series,* which she created in the early 1980s.

WOMEN OF FAITH™
loved
COLLECTION

Resources to remind you—or to encourage you to discover for the very first time—what God's grace and love mean for you.

Loved by God Devotional: Fifty-two weeks of inspiration with messages from Women of Faith speakers, remarkable real-life stories from event attendees, and insights from some of the freshest voices speaking to women today.

Loved Journal: Record your thoughts, prayers, and dreams on the lined pages in this beautiful journal. Features quotes from Women of Faith speakers and friends, plus encouraging Scriptures to inspire reflection and personal insights.

You Are Loved Bible Study: Discover the everlasting love God has for you in this eight-week Bible study. Includes daily activities, weekly challenges, and suggested Bible verses to commit to memory.

Loved: The Farewell Tour DVD: Bring home the event of a lifetime to enjoy again and again. Recorded *live* at the 2015 Women of Faith tour, this two-disc DVD set features powerful messages from some of America's best-loved speakers.

Learn more at WomenofFaith.com.

CP0906

women of faith

For twenty years . . . in cities across North America . . . Women of Faith has been connecting with millions of women to share this message: "God loves you and is crazy about you!"

Long before reality TV, Women of Faith speakers were candidly sharing their real problems and challenges in life. Their courageous stories welcomed women into a circle of friends, showed them they were not alone, and offered reassurance that wherever they are in life, Jesus is right there with them.

Women of Faith points women to the truths in the Bible that bring comfort, redemption, forgiveness, confidence, challenge, reassurance, and hope.

For more information about Women of Faith events, inspiration, and encouragement, visit WomenofFaith.com.

CF0905